Choosing to Float

To my tribe, the pieces of my shipwreck that kept me afloat.

To George, who was and always will be, the main reason that I breathe.

and to Ian, my happiness

Revelation 21:4

'He will wipe every tear from their eyes. There will be no more death or mourning or crying or pain, for the old order of things has passed away'.

CONTENTS

PART IV: LEARNING TO ADAPT

ACKNOWLEDGMENTS

To all my friends and family without whom Family Campbell would not have weathered the storm: thank you.

To the 'Wives of GBM' Facebook group, the strongest people I know and who in turn gave me strength: thank you.

To Louisa, Tash, Penny, and Rachel – my friends, I don't need to say more: thank you.

To The Rev. David Baker, whose love, support, and pastoral care never wavered: thank you.

To Dr. Tim Harrower, the best of the very best and who will always have my eternal gratitude: thank you.

To the Oncology Team at Royal Devon and Exeter Hospital, our South Molton GPs, North Devon Hospice, the District, Out of Hours and Paramedic teams who held us safely for over a decade: thank you.

To Karen, because your soul is full of light and I love you. You are one of the strongest people I know: thank you.

To my parents, who have walked beside us in our valley of shadow, who I couldn't have reached the other side without: thank you.

To Mum, Sarah, Sue, JK, and Andrew for their proof-reading and words of wisdom (I was never offended!): thank you.

To Jill, who has painted my memories for the past fifteen years and who has, yet again, produced an amazing work of art for my book: thank you.

To Ian, George, and our wonderful boys, you are my world and my blessing, you have helped me find joy again: thank you.

But my main thank you is to David, in heaven, without who this book would not exist: May you rest in peace my darling man: thank you for letting me love you and for loving me in return. .

FOREWORD

It's amazing how one moment in time can change the whole course of your life. How one event can make the bottom drop out of your world. How one conversation, in one sterile room, can take away the last shred of remaining hope that you had been clinging on to. How the look of sympathy and compassion in a stranger's eyes as they deliver hideous news to you can take your breath away. Only to then find yourself telling *them* that "everything is ok" in a meagre attempt to try and make it right for them; offering them the forgiveness they seek for hurting you.

And then you leave the room to gather the shattered remains of your dreams and piece them back together... after thanking the doctor for their time.

After we were told that David's disease would kill him we were amazed of the number of people that knew someone and every book seemed to have a character with the same condition. Each time I turned on the television there was a character in a plot, a special feature on Young Doctors, and David's surgeon was even followed in a BBC documentary. We went from blissful ignorance to not being able to outrun this beast that stalked our every move, which was there, just over our shoulder. A presence that we could never hide from nor outrun.

The horsehair holding up our Sword of Damocles held firm for thirteen years. Sometimes it slipped and the sword dropped and hovered just above our heads. But every time it got closer and each time our fear grew, our ability to cope decreased. Our smiles became more brittle and our peace more tenuous; our fear grew.

But we were lucky, we had faith which brings hope and belief in the afterlife; where love triumphs and are our souls are cleansed. Over the years my thoughts on faith changed and I grew to appreciate that all faiths are grounded in the same underlying principles of love, peace, joy, beauty, and hospitality. I found myself gently encouraging the people I encountered to be on a journey of faith, to be held by a higher being, to understand there is a purpose. To hold hope gently.

Afterwards, I tried to erect a barrier against further hurt for both me and our son, which was a daily battle that left me emotionally exhausted. 'Is that all you have got to worry about?' ricocheted around my brain until my perspective seemed distorted and the balance of what was normal forever displaced; resentment of those whose life seemed perfect burned like acid.

Resilience is a funny thing; we talk about how exposing our children to challenges will grow their resilience. But how much should we, or our children, be exposed to? How many challenges should we face before our characters, personalities, our very souls are changed and twisted beyond recognition, without any way forward or path of return?

And then we face the choice: to go down or to go up; to be fearful or to have faith; to be drawn towards the dark or walk into the light; to drown or to float.

I chose to float.

.

Part I
The Beginning

Chapter One
THE DIAGNOSIS

I will start at the beginning…

David and I married in September 2007 in All Saints Church, North Molton, Devon, surrounded by friends and family. It still remains one of the happiest days of my life; it was an amazing day. I'm sure it's been said a million times before to a million different couples, but we were told that no-one had ever seen a couple more in love. Our road stretched ahead paved with our dreams. We were blessed.

David was a simple soul who grew up in Newtownabbey, Northern Ireland, surrounded by his family, his church, and his friends. People meant everything to him: he was man that loved his family and friends, a man that liked sport – playing, coaching, and watching. He was a man that loved to be at home, always waiting with a gin and tonic for when I whistled in the door after a long day in a stressful job. David never felt threatened by my drive and my need to fly. He was my rock and my inspiration. There was always a word to calm or encourage me, to sympathise or correct. I can't put into words how his quiet strength gave me my confidence to realise the dreams I had for my career.

But my role in a Phase I Clinical Research Unit in Leeds wasn't conducive to starting a family and so we chose to move back home to north Devon, where I grew up and where we would be closer to my parents. Both David and I worked in clinical research, both specialising in oncology (cancer) clinical trials. Our life was perfect: one (relatively!) well-behaved spaniel, Brandy, one house in the country, one set of shared dreams. David loved to shop at the local market and go for walks, and I liked to work and drink wine! We lived in our perfect world with each other. The only thing that would make things more perfect would be a baby, but we weren't in a rush. God would let things happen at the right time.

Shortly after we moved to Devon, David started to say that he could smell gas, which was weird as I couldn't, and we didn't have gas in the house. We didn't really pay much attention to it, but David went to the doctor just to be on the safe side. Nothing was deemed to be sinister and so we didn't worry about it. After all, how could anything possibly be wrong as we were both in hideously good health.

Everything changed one night as I woke up about 2am to David having a seizure; one of those shocking ones that I had only seen on the television before. I had absolutely no idea what was going on, but I knew that I had to keep him safe and try and avoid him hurting himself and not depress his tongue. I remember shouting at him, trying desperately to bring him back to me with willpower and love, but it had no effect. David was grey, his body contorted and in rigor, he had wet himself and had bitten his tongue. The blood had mixed with saliva and it was smeared down his cheek and over the bed, which was a morbid trail of his movements. Seeing any person in a seizure is a scary thing and watching David foaming at the mouth and shouting strange, guttural noises was something that I never got used to. I knew I had to call an ambulance which was a challenge in itself as it was before the time when people carried their mobiles with them everywhere. I had to decide whether to go and get the phone or stay with David as he seized. I made the call. The wonderful person at the end of the phone told me the ambulance was on the way and calmed me. By the time David's seizure finished he was on the floor and, as a dead weight, he was too large for me to lift so I covered him and left him there.

In the same way that there is stillness after a storm, once David was asleep on the floor a quietness descended on the house and I stood next to a window watching for the ambulance. In the distance was a flashing blue light. I watched the ambulance travel along the opposite side of the valley, disappear out of sight to cross the bridge over the River Taw and then up, out of the village and down our winding lane. I went outside so they didn't go passed the entrance to our courtyard. The relief of seeing green clad, capable professionals is one of the most welcome sights in the world. For all you paramedics and ambulance crew out there, you have no idea of the intense relief when you know you can abdicate responsibility, just for a little while and know that the person that you love is in the best hands. It's funny, it doesn't really matter what is going on, but I never got over the feeling that our situation was serious enough to merit calling 999 and ask for an ambulance. David was disorientated when he came round and I remember being distinctly uneasy to see him going to the toilet, naked, in front of the paramedics without a care in the world. They rushed to reassure me that this loss of inhibitions was quite a common occurrence after seizures. However, David seemed to be getting back to his normal self and, after observing him for a while, we agreed that (the now snoring heavily) David, didn't need to be disturbed further and we would go to the surgery to get some follow ups done later that day.

Waking up the next morning was a slightly surreal experience. David didn't understand why he was on a towel and why there was blood on the bedding and the carpet. It appeared that he had no recollection of what had happened. And this, in a way, was a comfort. If he couldn't remember, then it obviously couldn't have been that bad and he seemed fine that morning. Suddenly, the happenings of the night before seemed very surreal. So, we started the exploration with no real concerns. After visiting the doctors, we went to A&E for further tests…nothing. So, it was agreed the best course of action was to get booked in for an MRI scan in a couple of weeks. We went home and carried on with our life, slightly perturbed but still completely oblivious of what was going on. We both went back to work in the afternoon.

David was called for the MRI a couple of weeks later and then, after the scan, was called to go for another scan with a contrast agent the following day. On reflection, this is when alarms bells should have started to ring (especially with us both working in oncology studies) but we were still so naïve, and so confident that nothing could happen to us.

The day we got the news, we were called back to the local hospital where an appointment had been arranged with a cardiologist. We were shown to what seems like a room in the bowels of the hospital and didn't look like a normal consulting room – almost like we'd been slotted in somewhere, just so we could be seen. I remember the consultant apologising for the delay in us being seen as he had been on holiday. We were fine with that…after all everyone needs a break! The cardiologist proceeded to show us scans of David's brain where a tumour had been found, which was quite large, 7cm x 5cm x 4cm and was in his left frontal lobe. An appointment was being made for us to see an oncologist in Plymouth who would be able to explain more and give us some treatment options.

We left totally shell-shocked. How on earth should we process that information? How should we tell people? Now, with the benefit of years, I look back on us just being so young. David was 26 years old; he was healthy, and he was sporty for heaven's sake. We believed there would be options, and we would be ok.

Telling people was just strange and they fell into three camps: those who suspected it might have been a tumour and were ready to hear bad things; those that knew of David's seizure but didn't expect a tumour; and those that knew nothing but needed to be told. The last group were the hardest to a certain extent – that complete blindside piece of information that left those on the other end of the phone speechless. And that silence was always filled with traditionally British platitudes and reassurance. I'm a big one for getting it out there and doing the right thing. My default position was to make sure no-one gets upset or offended so this meant that I had to make sure everyone knew. If we told X, then Y needed to be told as well.

I learned that sharing news has several purposes: it makes it real for you; it helps you gauge reaction to validate your own; and it creates your support network. However, it is a double-edged sword as it seemed like hundreds of people wanted to be told personally: family; friends; church; my work; David's work; and old school friends. This is lovely but exhausting, and I was left emotionally drained and wrung out. Over time I learned that if people didn't understand I was doing my best and chose to get offended, then that is their decision. Our true friends and family were those that understood that I made mistakes, forgot birthdays, missed them off email or text updates…and they didn't mind. In fact, those that really understood me recognised that mistakes like that were warning flags that I wasn't coping and knew to pull me in close to protect me. But this frantic chain of communication also meant that I didn't get time to process the information. I could repeat, explain, clarify for others, but the processing of what this meant for me and my life didn't really happen. To this day, I am not sure whether this was a blessing or a curse; but what is done is done and I must let it be.

The day of the Plymouth appointment arrived, and it was a 'big trip'. Plymouth is about two hours from us, and my parents came up trumps telling us that Dad would take us as we would be hearing things that we needed to discuss on the way home and they didn't want me driving. Mum made us a packed lunch and Dad told us to sit in the back and he said he wasn't going to talk on the way home and he didn't want to interfere. He said that David and I would need to talk things through as a married couple. My Dad is an inveterate advice-giver and loves nothing more than to start a sentence with 'what you want to do is…' so this was a massive effort on his part, and we were very grateful. I remember us both sitting in the back of the car clutching each other's hand and staring out of our respective windows, trying desperately to be brave and not to cry; those hot emotional tears that can't be held back. We had no idea what we were going to hear.

7

But the news we heard was better than we thought it would be as the tumour was a grade II* astrocytoma. Yes, the tumour would eventually kill David but not for many years. Happy days. We had options and one was surgery to excise as much tumour as possible, or we could just leave it alone and scan regularly to watch for any changes. Throughout the meeting I was taking notes as I just knew I wouldn't retain all the information, and over the years it became a bit of a joke for us. Due to the nature of the tumour, its size and location, we left with a referral to one of the leading brain surgeons in the UK, at The National Hospital in London.

The journey home was surreal, having been ready for immediate action, chemotherapy, radiotherapy, surgery, but being told we didn't need to do those was a shock. It was almost like an anti-climax as the battle we had prepared ourselves for was suddenly dissipated. Being told (after we asked) that the tumour would be the cause of David's death, but for an undisclosed number of years was just strange. How many people at 26 know what the cause of their death will be? However, our optimism started to grow again. It's not all bad, in fact this is a blessing, how many people get this chance to really love life and to appreciate it for what it is? We decided that we would go for the surgery – after all, if 80% of the tumour was taken that's 80% less of a tumour to progress. Surely that was worth it. Surely the benefits outweighed the risks.

After the oncology consultation we went into a period of adjustment but the appointments didn't stop as David needed to get his epilepsy controlled and make sure everything was stabilised. This is when we met Doctor Tim Harrower, one of the most wonderful physicians we have ever met and someone that we came to rely on as a source of truth and pragmatism. David mourned the loss of driving as he missed going to the golfing range, the market, and taking Brandy to the beach to walk. I was catapulted into world that I didn't want to be in: It wasn't my job to drive or go shopping. But we adjusted as we had no choice. We started to learn the best places

Most tumours are graded from I to IV, I being the least serious and IV being the most serious.

to park at hospitals, what the car parking charges were, the quickest way to the consulting rooms, where the toilets were, and soon we were walking the local hospital corridors as if we worked there. We knew we needed to phone to check prescriptions had been sent to the pharmacy and that the pharmacy had processed them. We understood that we weren't the only patients that doctors saw, and we needed to repeat things as they seldom had time to read notes. We knew that David's notes or results from different institutions would rarely arrive before him. None of this phased or frustrated us: it is just how it is…busy people in busy hospitals in a busy world.

We learned that you can fight changes and get annoyed about them, you can be frustrated, and you can hate them. However, change will always happen and sometimes it is easier to let them wash over you and to go with the flow. You get tired fighting against the tide – there is a lot more peace to be found lying on your back and letting the waves carry you. We learned that you can either get out the other side, slightly bedraggled and a little the worse for wear, or you can drag yourself out exhausted, beaten, and depressed.

We learned to choose our battles.

We chose to float.

Chapter Two
MORE NEWS

Life continued, we worked, and we relaxed at weekends. David was out playing golf with Dad in early May, and whilst he was away, I carried on doing some painting in our house. The radio was on in the background, and I was up step ladders singing 'Stand by your Man' at the top of my voice (I have no other volume as my family will attest!) when I started to cry, fairly uncontrollably, quickly replaced by me laughing at myself as it was very unlike me to give in to emotion like that. I didn't really think anything of it and just laughed with David about it when he got home.

But the next day, I woke and my breasts were sore….in amongst all this hideousness we had forgotten the possibility that I might be pregnant! However, the weird emotion and the sore breasts gave us enough cause to crack open a pregnancy test and yes, it was positive. I remember the day clearly: it was a Sunday at the start of May and we were preparing to go to church. I remember walking up the church path, face beaming to be met by our vicar at the church door where I couldn't contain my joy (there was no waiting the customary twelve weeks for me!) But the miracle was that we had stopped trying for a baby as after David's seizure and then after the diagnosis, all thoughts of a baby disappeared. So after nearly two years it was a amazing that I conceived when I did and we worked out that I must have fallen pregnant the week before David's seizure (I can even pinpoint the time as I had had my feet up against the headboard messaging a good friend and colleague on my laptop and she was laughing that we had resorted to going to bed at lunchtime to keep ourselves on schedule!)

David and I had several appointments in London with his brain surgeon and the upshot was that we would wait until after the birth to have the operation. Not too long as we needed to take some action, but we wanted David to see our baby, just in case the unspeakable happened and we also wanted to enjoy the pregnancy. So, our first life changing decision was made. I was due mid-January and we would go for David's craniotomy in late March. Decision made; we got back to normal life.

And life *was* normal, we were both working, and David's health was good. Nothing else untoward had happened and we entered a joyful period of preparation. And I absolutely loved being pregnant and really bloomed (probably because of less wine!) David was so looking forward to being a father and I loved the idea of a mini-Campbell that was going to make our family a complete unit: David, me, the baby and our gorgeous, most wonderful dog, Brandy. Despite the tumour, our lives were happy and complete; we were tucked away in our cottage in Devon completely happy and in love. I went to the local pregnancy group and met Louisa, who was also having her first baby, and we found friendship – laughing over pregnancy and, later, holding each other up when we were reeling with the complete exhaustion of the first few months with a newborn. My cousin Jane bought me oil to stop stretch marks, and every evening David would rub it into my bump and then, in the last trimester, track a pen torch across my tummy in the dark and then feel the baby move inside me. We bonded as a family. I never did get stretch marks.

During this time, David was very chilled about things. We were lucky with the position of his tumour; he didn't get anxious or depressed, his personality didn't change, and he only had a few other physical symptoms. David carried on working and visited hospitals in the UK and Europe with his work which involved helping to train clinical teams on how to run oncology clinical studies. There were changes because he couldn't drive, and we were working to get his epilepsy completely controlled. David's company were wonderful at helping us make the necessary adaptations. Considering we were in rural north Devon his company and manager were extremely supportive. Yes, you could say that David was due the adaptations, but support, in whatever form it takes, is so very gratefully received.

David and I used to play a game; it was up to me to guess when he was having a (focal) seizure and it was up to him to try and mask it. If I guessed right, he was very annoyed with himself, and I suppose it was all part of him helping himself to continue his life. On occasion he would return home a little despondent and tired. I particularly remember when he told me that, whilst doing some training, he'd had to leave the room as he was having a seizure that he couldn't control. I was so upset with him and got quite annoyed; why would he leave a room with medics to go and stand in a corridor when help and support was right in front of him? Who would mind knowing that his brain tumour had given him epilepsy? But David wanted to carry on with his life and I needed to respect that.

David started working on a new oncology study around this time and one of the study hospitals was Exeter. The main physician leading the team was also David's oncologist. It always gave me comfort to know that David was in safe hands when he was visiting Exeter (as he was with any of the hospitals to be honest). Clinical trials have always been an important part of our world and David took part in a couple of observational clinical studies in London to check out his brain function and to see how it affected his cognition. These results were amazing as David had actually displaced some of his left hemisphere activity (reading and speech) to the right hemisphere so that his brain could cope; this was simply amazing to us. The brain tumour had also displaced David's maths function but had not infiltrated that area so David, to his dying day, remained remarkably sharp with numbers, which was incredible as David had achieved a first degree in Maths and Computing. Thank God for small mercies.

Although life continued and on the whole we were happy, David wasn't a saint and did get upset about things (who wouldn't?) but it was me that was angry about why this should happen to him. I used to get frustrated that David didn't seem bothered by the actual tumour and the injustice of it all. On one occasion I shouted at him why on earth did this have to happen to him? His answer stays with me to this day: 'God's given me this tumour because He knows I can cope with it'.

The deep bedrock of David's faith was a saving factor for us on many occasions and something we both clung to. That feeling that something or someone is holding you and watching for you was always a source of comfort for us as it meant someone was in control of a situation that we couldn't possibly control. All I can liken it to is unmovable situations that we have no control over: we can't change the weather; I couldn't *make* myself get pregnant; and you can't stop the bolt of lightning hitting. Trusting in God is like that; someone else is in control, you just need to accept and trust that the right thing will happen.

On the other hand, I wanted to try and wrestle some level of control over the uncontrollable. I might not be able to change things, but I could do what I could to help. So, I read about diets, exercise, meditation, and mindfulness, yoga…you name it. I was prepared to give it a go – or more precisely, I was prepared to make David give it a go! I created diet sheets of allowed foods and ideal meals, and of what David needed to eat on a daily basis. For a man that loved chocolates and crisps (don't, it was galling, he could eat anything and not put on an ounce!) this was hard. He did not want to swap his treats for turmeric and green tea, so we reached a compromise; we would change as much as we could but not let it rule our lives. Mindfulness was a 'yes' for me but a 'no' for David.

Looking back, David was wonderful for letting me run with everything I wanted to do as it was completely against his personality. He was so laid back he was almost horizontal, but he let me express myself in the way that I always did, by planning and executing; after all, I am a project manager by trade! Equilibrium was achieved and it gave me some notion of being in control.

What I also did was something that every single physician advised against; I sought advice and knowledge from Doctor Google, which something I am now firmly against. It has its purposes when you know what you are looking for, but the random searches by a person with limited knowledge and a lot of power is, quite frankly, dangerous. I would caution against late night searches, seeking advice when you wake up at 2am and sleep eludes you, when you are tired after a long week or, as I found out after George was born, when wine is involved! What you are likely to read is not going to give comfort and may well do more harm than good. I speak as though I am coming from a position of enlightenment, and I am, relatively … but being enlightened doesn't make you perfect and Doctor Google and I maintained an on/off relationship spanning over a decade.

Chapter Three
THE START OF THE JOURNEY

I don't think my life has had a more turbulent time than the first three months of 2010. Our baby was due on 10th January 2010, and on top of the normal baby planning, we had planned David's operation.

The whole of the UK was under the grip of a particularly bitter winter, and we were snowed in from 10th to 13th January. However, there was no movement on the baby front, much to my great annoyance. I was *never* late for *anything* and tramping through the snow to get some exercise with David encouraging me to walk in his footsteps was not an incredible amount of fun. However, on the 14th our midwife got through the snow to our house and (basically) told us to have sex that night as that would start things rolling. Laughing she left us with a wave and a smile telling us that she would see us later. We were having a home birth. Never one to ignore a positive course of action, David and I duly got to it that evening and went to sleep happily. I woke at around 2am and my waters had broken. Joy! I told David to stay in bed and I wandered upstairs – we lived in an upside-down house - with a good book and settled in whilst texting the midwife that the pain was 'fine' and no problems at all; oh how very, very naïve I was.

When David got up around 6am we started timing contractions

and I was quite close together so we messaged the midwife again who said she would mobilise the troops and to get the water bath run. David ran the water bath. Our midwife stayed with us, and another midwife came with a student – all good. Around 9am they said it was time for me to get in but when they tested the water it was cold. David had put his hand in to test it, but the hot water was at the top and the cold water was underneath. However, come hell or high water (no pun intended!), I was getting in that bath and no-one was to tell David what was up.

And this is how David had changed. He did everything to the best of his ability, but the ability was that of a grown child. He didn't quite grasp the full picture in the way he would have done before becoming ill. I was in that cold bath for hours and no amount of hot water was going to get it to where it needed to be; our hot water tank in the old barn conversion wasn't up to it. The midwives were saying that it was not the best idea but I was not moving and David was never to know. I sat in that bath for about six hours. My time in the water bath was quite funny: we had some wine delivered; a grocery shop; a travel cot delivery; some builders stopped to ask directions; and the postman popped in to say hello!

After about eighteen hours of labour the baby was starting to get distressed and my contractions were still two minutes apart, and so I was taken to hospital. After an epidural – brief nod of apology to the two male doctors standing at the bottom of my bed discussing which was the best pain relief option for me who I bellowed at that I didn't care which option they go for, but they needed to do it now (it might have come across as rude, not sure) – George arrived late on the 15th January 2010 and, as David couldn't drive home, and we were allowed to stay together in the labour suite. This was a blessing as it gave us time to bond as a family.

David's love for George was immediate and a wonder to witness. His whole face softened when he held George, and it was obvious that he was born to be a father. My parents came to take us home the next day and David got lost amongst the flurry of car seats, where people were going to sit, how to strap George in and which was the best way to go home. What should have been a proud moment for David – taking his new family home - was completely surpassed, and he receded into the background. However, when we got home, Mum and Dad soon left us knowing that we needed time to settle. David, being David, took it all in his stride.

David was an amazing father and we launched straight out into the new world, taking George and Brandy to the beach and to church before George was two weeks old, and we were out walking most days. David was into nappy changing, bathing and generally being wonderful. But, after the birth, my thoughts immediately went onto preparation for the next thing in our life; a trip to Northern Ireland to see David's family before heading to London for his surgery.

I don't think I ever had a time to come to terms with accepting and adjusting to motherhood. Quite a few people had said to me about the love that you feel for your children as soon as they were born so I was expecting a tidal wave of love to hit me. I thought I was going to be a natural mother; bonding immediately, breast feeding and loving maternity leave. Instead, I found the baby groups difficult as they weren't my thing. They sapped my time and I had no patience listening to mothers talk about how wonderful motherhood was as if they had all the time in the world. It grated on me. But my friendship with Louisa was growing in strength and we met Tash in a baby communication group, which was another friendship that grew to be so important to me over the years. My underlying feeling was that George was another person that I needed to protect, that I had responsibility for. It was almost as if I couldn't afford to let myself be in love with him because I needed to devote my time to make things right for him and keep him, and his father, safe.

Don't get me wrong, I loved my son beyond belief, and I would annihilate anyone that harmed a hair on his head, but the luxury of enjoying that love and, indeed, enjoying George, was not there. I only really started to feel 'in love' with George when he learned to walk, and when that pleasure and surge of love came, I couldn't keep the smile from my face. It was that smile, that feeling, which David had from the moment George was born.

But I digress.

We flew to Northern Ireland in March, and I found the trip difficult. I was a new mother and coming to terms with my emotions. George was less than two months old; I'd weaned George onto expressed milk, David's operation was coming up and there were an awful lot of people to see over the weekend. Whilst we were there, I finalised travel plans with my family about where we were going to stay in London and managed a myriad of administrative and medical enquiries. It was all very overwhelming for me, but I tried not to let it show. I am not sure how successful I was.

And this was the pattern that we settled in to: David was protected from any stress as we had been told that he would do better if he remained in an emotionally stable condition and I ran our lives. Consequently, so much of my life was played out behind a curtain. I was like the proverbial swan: serene above the surface but paddling frantically underneath.

But David loved every minute of his visit home, and I was so glad we had made the journey.

Ironically, we would make a very similar trip back eleven years later and it is amazing the difference I felt between the two, with the benefit of age and hindsight. Instead of focusing on my internal worries and to do lists, I learned to look outwards, to look at what others were experiencing and find the joy in the moment. Practical concerns were always there, whether it was a bill to pay, a boiler service to arrange, how to get George to do his homework (and tell me what parent doesn't have that challenge!) or to follow up on tests and prescriptions. As the years went on I learned not to let those worries cloud my vision and perspective and I learned how to compartmentalise so that I could focus on the important things in life. It was a very slow and arduous road.

And after our trip to Northern Ireland, we came home and prepared for hospital.

Part II
The During

Chapter Four
LONDON

After leaving George with my parents, David and I took the train to London and headed towards my cousin's flat, where I would be staying during our time there. To get to David to the hospital it was about a forty minute tube ride with a change, but it was completely doable and we were very grateful. The night before David's admission was strange... probably the same feeling you get before a big exam or an important match – we were both churned up and at a loose end, just wanting to get there and get started. It was a feeling that we would come to understand and accept. It was the same before a consultation to hear results - the scans or tests meant nothing - but the night before results was always a quieter, more nerve-jangling time.

The National Hospital is a beautiful old building on Queen's Square in London; it has an ornate chapel and endless long corridors and you can almost hear the characters from centuries past. David was admitted on 28th March 2010, and we were left to ourselves in David's room. We laid on his bed, snuggled up together watching the final week of the cooking programme, Masterchef. I have very fond memories of the 'final three' – Dhruv, Alex, and Tim – from the 2010 series and, even now, love seeing them come back to judge. Insignificant to most, but I found many such moments became the tapestry that was our life together and, even now, a chance to reconnect with the past. I left the hospital late, promising to arrive first thing the next morning.

David was due to go down to theatre early for his operation as it was a long procedure and there would be MRI scans throughout to monitor progress. As David's tumour was a diffused it meant that there were no clear lines to take the tumour away. The way I understood it in my mind was that it was like a jelly. If you make a red jelly and let it set completely, you can then pour a yellow jelly on it and a defined line is created between the two. If you want to eat the yellow jelly, then it is easier to scrape if off along the join. However, if you pour the yellow jelly onto the red before it is set then the yellow penetrates into some of the red and it becomes orange. You then can't separate the two. That's how David's tumour was: tumour matter had invaded the healthy brain tissue and there was no chance of removing the tumour without taking the healthy tissue away, and therefore some of David's brain function.

I arrived at the hospital early, in time to see David have his checks and talk to the surgical team about the procedure and what was going to happen throughout the day. His room was literally buzzing with doctors, nurses, therapists, care assistants, machines. David was on the bed and in his eyes was a look that I came to know and every time I saw it my heart squeezed, the air went out of my lungs and my soul was crying out to his. He was like a trapped animal in a cage that he didn't know how he got there or how to get out. He was completely helpless. Looking back this must have been a turning point in our relationship: that was the first time that I felt I needed to protect him, to take over everything and stop his pain. From an emotional aspect, all I could do was look, tell him I loved him and that he would be ok, to hold his hand and let him know that I would always be here for him. But practically I could take over: I could make sure tests were done on time, medication prescribed, results obtained. It gave me a job. It made me feel useful. It gave me some control.

David's bed was wheeled out of his room early in the morning and I was left, bereft, in a cold empty room that suddenly was a vacuum, where the life had been sucked out of it. And I stayed there all day, not eating, drinking, or moving. I had brought a cross stitch tapestry and I sat, in a chair by the window, stitching and praying. The hours ticked by. Occasionally a member of the ward team would pop in and check that I was ok and say that he would be a while yet and suggested that I go for a walk. But I wasn't going anywhere as, if I was needed, I was going to be right there, where I could get to David in moments. As it started to get dark, I started to worry, where was he? Why wasn't I getting any news? I asked at the nurse's station but there was no news. It is a very fine line between verging on neurotic and feeling like you are being forgotten about during these moments. Perhaps they have been too busy to let you know something? Perhaps everyone thinks that someone else has updated you? So, I kept popping out and trying to keep the edge out of my voice. Eventually I was told that he was due in recovery shortly…but 'shortly' came and went. Trying to keep panic at bay when you are tired and have lost perspective of time is one of the challenges that anyone waiting for a loved one to come from surgery will have experienced. I had created two messaging groups (it was in the days when you had to text people) so that I could keep everyone updated and I was sporadically messaging to say that there were no updates. Finally, I remember just crying saying that someone must know something that they could tell me, and I was reassured that I would be the first to know. So, I went back to my soulless room and waited, tapestry put aside.

I don't remember the final time when the team told me I could see him, and I don't remember how long it took us to walk there. But I do remember seeing my wonderful husband propped up in bed with his head heavily bandaged. He saw me and smiled, and I knew he recognised me. When I got up to him, he called me Karen, his sister's name. I didn't mind then and during the intervening years have come to recognise what an honour that was as Karen is the most truly wonderful person and sister to me. He then started to wave his arms around and told me that he was playing golf. I couldn't help but smile. I didn't feel alarm or concern, after all he had just had brain surgery…he was never going to hop out of bed and tell me he was ready for home.

I went home and slept.

David's surgeon was an early bird with his ward round at around 6:30am. I missed him the day after David's surgery so I resolved to get up and get the tube at 5:30am in future so I knew I would be there in time. Again, a pattern that I never stopped – I was always there for ward rounds if humanly possible and stayed until the evening. At the end of the day I would collapse exhausted into a taxi to take me home, with my parents coming up trumps again as they'd offered to pay for taxis to take some of the burden off me – it's the little things that meant so much. David's recovery was remarkable, the day after he was up and walking, the day after that the physio had him up and down stairs. He was slightly confused, and I had to help him with words and sentences, and he still got me confused with Karen, but I could live with all of that. David had got through the operation. We were in a good place.

A few days post-surgery we had a visit in the day as the histology results were back, and it was not good news. David's tumour was in fact a grade III anaplastic astrocytoma. When we got home David would need to start radiotherapy. I found out later that the course of radiotherapy that David had was the most aggressive that he could have, and this ruled out any future radiotherapy. A grade III tumour is life-limiting and we were told that David would probably have less than ten years to live.

I can't describe that feeling when you think you have got there, you've done the hard work, but victory was literally snatched from our grasp. We went from feeling elated to dejected, but also not quite sure what was happening – it was too strange. The medical team must have weighed up when to tell us as David was still quite fragile. But we accepted it, we had no choice. I remember going back to the flat, that evening and I had arranged to meet with my other cousin, Jane, who was getting married later that year. Her mother, Julie, was down in London as they had been wedding dress shopping. I walked over to her flat and I just remember trying not to get too upset as it was such a special day for them. I tried and failed. And they were lovely. It just goes to show how different people's worlds are and how joy can run parallel to sadness, certainty with ambiguity. It also helped me to understand that you can share in other's joy even when you are walking in your own valley of shadow. That it is ok to feel joy at the same time as despair, one doesn't counteract the other, diminish the other, nor make the other disappear. Life is about balance and perspective, a series of moments where there are both transient and more deeply embedded emotions.

David and I experienced unparalleled love and support when we were in hospital, about ten days in total. Tracey, another cousin, sent a Fortnum and Mason's hamper, full of wonderful nibbles and treats, and friends dropped in to say hello. David had always been quite proud of his hair and hated seeing half his head shaved and so Jane, brought us in hair clippers and David went grade 2 all over. Jane, also knowing that David was struggling with word recall, bought us a game called 'Who's Naked?' For those children of the 1980's, we had a popular game called 'Guess Who?' where you had to ask questions about what the person looked like to see if you could guess who the other person got. Well, this was the same, but the people had no clothes on…. you can guess the rest. Well, this helped David's word recall immensely!

David was also encouraged to leave the hospital and one beautiful day David and I set out across Queen's Square, Russell Square and then went into The National History Museum. We were delighted with ourselves that we had got out. But we had overstretched David who got tired, so we sat in the main hall of museum and watched the world go by. After a while we set off back to the hospital but we got lost and I had no idea how to get back (again, this was before smart phones). The only thing I could think of was to get a black cab so I hailed one down and the driver was explaining to me that it was just around the corner, but by that time David was really flagging and I really didn't care if it was fifty metres or fifty miles. Luckily the London cabbie was lovely and he took us 'home' to the hospital. By this time, we were very good friends with the ward staff and were chastised teasingly for our mistake! But we tried and to try is better than to be too fearful to give it a go. This didn't put us off and a couple of days later we met Jane and her fiancé Kingsley and went for a drink in the local pub across Queen Square Gardens. Whilst we were there having a laugh David's brain surgeon came in…we almost hid under the table…to this day I am not sure if he noticed us!

Easter came and went and it was George's first Easter and we missed it. We had been in London around ten days and were talking to the team about David being discharged. Then one day David had had enough, he wanted to go home, and he wanted to go home now. The plan was for Dad to come to London to get us, but we had no time for that. I hadn't even packed my bag, but David got discharged and we went to the flat, David stayed in the taxi, and I packed up and then we went off to Paddington. I was absolutely petrified as David still had the staples in his head and a bandage. I sat him in the main Paddington foyer and went to buy train tickets. We took the first train home. David, being David, insisted on sitting on the aisle and his tumour side was on the outside. He wouldn't move. As people were walking up and down the carriage, all we needed was one stumble or bump and we would have been in trouble. The journey home kept me in a high level of anxiety, and it was something that never happened again. I learned to be dominant about situations that didn't feel right in my gut. If I had to deal with these situations that were not of my choosing, well I would deal with them in the best way that I knew how and keep the risk as low as possible.

Overall, the whole craniotomy experience in London was amazing though, David's care had been first class and his recovery was swift and without any hitches. When we got home our neighbours had set out a banner saying 'Welcome Home David' – it's all about love and support.

Chapter Five
BACK IN THE REAL WORLD

The National Hospital was a bubble in which we had lived; a sterile, supported, and protected world. When we got home, it was like someone had ripped the bandages off. We had been told that David might have panic attacks and that he shouldn't be exposed to too much noise because it would bring on headaches. We were also trying to maintain the emotional stability. Welcome to the world of a new-born baby, a household where two salaries had dropped to statutory pay and, again, that flurry of appointments and calls to set up radiotherapy schedules and lifts. It didn't really tick the boxes of a relaxed and stable household.

I was also finding maternity leave difficult. I felt that I had played my part; I had got David to hospital, seen him through the operation, got him home and helped him sort out treatment schedules. I was now left, literally, holding the baby as David had made a good cognitive recovery and was on a phased return to work. I was jealous, I wanted to be at work, it just wasn't in my nature to not work, and my work validates who I am. The plan had changed: David was the paternal one and the deal had been that he was the homemaker, and I was the worker. That's who David and Clare were; that's how we rolled. I can remember one day, standing in George's nursery ironing a white wash when David came back in from his office and shouting

'I can't fucking stand this anymore! I am not cut out for this!' Long discussions ensued and we agreed that I would go back to work part-time and Mum offered to have George on one day and we would have a childminder three days a week. I have a photograph in our baby album of David feeding George and I am at my laptop working. Normality was restored. I have learned over the years to disregard the raised eyebrows of people that felt I should have been at home with George, that a mother's place is in the home. I learned that I could only deal with home if I had an escape, a release valve and that George was happier with a Mummy that wasn't as stressed. It was the right decision for our family, and I stand by it. If I could have chosen, I would have made myself more maternal, but you don't get to make those choices and there is very little point into trying to turn yourself into something you're not. I had bigger battles to fight.

David had started radiotherapy and was travelling to Exeter every weekday for about six weeks. He would be picked up early by a driver with a car full of people from north Devon heading to Exeter for radiotherapy and get home later the same day. They were long days for someone still in recovery from the craniotomy. He had a mask fitted so that his head was still when getting the radiotherapy. His head was burned on both sides where the radio went in and came out, and his hair started to fall out. I remember standing with him in front of the bathroom mirror both of us looking at each other in the mirror, David standing with a handful of hair hovering between his head and the sink. That same trapped look was in his eyes. The one that said: how have we got here? What has happened to my life? I did what I always did, offer love and support, a healthy dose of realism and practicality and then got us both to crack on. We either cracked on or crumbled apart, there was very little choice.

It was difficult for David to adjust to the new him: his head was misshapen on his left side, he had no hair on the left side of his head and little on the right, he had put on several stone with high dose steroids, his short-term memory was poor (especially for names) and his speech was slow. He still loved to go into town for a wander round though and loved the market. He used to get very upset with people staring at him and took to wearing a hat or cap. But, more difficult, were people that he knew crossing the street to avoid speaking to him. This was horrible at first and seemed so unnecessarily cruel. However, we came to understand that it was because people didn't know what to say or how to express themselves. How do you speak to a dying man who is only twenty-seven?

I look back and ask myself whether I gave him enough time to grieve for himself, for the man who was lost the minute that the scalpel cut open his head, the fact that he never felt the same way about himself. Did I understand enough? Did I listen when he needed me to? Did I really understand his own loss? Was I gentle in the face of his fear? I will never know the answers.

David had stayed at work for as long as he could after his operation but eventually the complexity and cognitive demands of his role, in combination with the responsibility the position held, meant that it wasn't sustainable for him, so his manager and I agreed, with David, that it would be better for him to stop work. It was a lot less stressful for him and placed the company in a safer position as running clinical trials carries with it a heavy burden of regulations and accountability.

It was a tough day when David stopped work as he lost part of his identity. I was just so relieved that the decision was made, and he was safe again. But for David, it was another nail in the coffin of his life. It was another thing that he loved stripped away. For when these decisions are made, they are very rarely reversed, even if there is the promise that this is not a binding decision at the time. And with that decision came more challenges for us. Each time I had a rant about work, he would look at me and sometimes, right in the depth of those eyes was a resentment which said: at least you can work. And what could be my response to that?

.

Chapter 6
GRIEVING

My grieving for David was never as bitter, raw, or real as those few months after we got back from London. I was grieving for the man that I married, the man that was changing in front of my eyes. I was devastated that my husband was being taken away from me and was slowly deteriorating. I didn't realise that David's brain was going to carry on dying for five years after his radiotherapy was complete. Our conversations lost their spark; we no longer really laughed together, we were friends, not lovers and I was his carer, not his companion. It didn't mean I loved him less, just differently. It didn't mean that I didn't want to be with him, it just meant that I had two children in the house and not one. David was still my rock, he was loving and dependable, he was trustworthy and a fabulous friend. But I lost my *person*. I was never going to get my wonderful man back. If I had known that, would I have argued against surgery? Would I have been happy to live in ignorance? Would we have opted for radiotherapy knowing that it would change him forever? Who knows. But I do know now that I would give anything now to have had the benefit of hindsight because I would have laughed louder, have loved more, said yes to everything, and seized every opportunity to be with the wonderful man that I had married before these irreversible changes occurred.

My head office was in Slough at the time and I used to travel to the office every couple of months, a journey of about three hours. In those three hours I would cry, big gulping sobs with hot emotional tears. I would cry until I could cry no more. I would hit the steering wheel, shout and swear. It was the only time that I really let myself go. Then, before I reached the office, I would park, patch up my makeup, brush my hair, and draw back behind the curtain of my life. I didn't allow myself (or others as far as humanly possible) to cry in front of David or George as they needed strength. There is also the feeling that once that lid came off there was no way that it was going to go back on. If people saw me cry then it would validate the appalling things that were happening to us. I didn't want anyone's pity, so I hid behind a façade of black humour and keeping busy. I didn't want the time to be alone with my thoughts as they were no friend of mine. I'm not saying that is right or wrong, healthy or unhealthy, but everyone finds their outlet and does what is best for them. That path of unrelenting activity remains in place today and I still don't think I have processed everything, I think there are years ahead of me, understanding piece by piece, what has happened to us.

David and I would talk about our future and all he wanted to do was get to forty. If he got there, then he wanted the biggest party filled with family and friends. It gave us something to aim for as he was turning forty in just over ten years. We always tried to look on the bright side and to identify things to look forward to for gave us alternative things to focus on. There is a guilt that comes with grief, that you will infect others with your grief or that you become a burden and that no-one really wants to hear your 'sob story'. We didn't know what was round the corner for us and how long David's illness would be for. My concern was that people will get bored of hearing about David so we hushed up our feelings as much as we could, only letting a few people in, and playing down the grief we were both experiencing. And I found Christmas to be the hardest and harshest time. Birthdays I could cope with but Christmas was when the whole world appeared to be celebrating and everyone was meant to be happy. David loved Christmas, and I mean *loved* Christmas. He did the Christmas jumpers, loved having people round, sung the Christmas songs, danced around the kitchen island, carried out the same traditions. And every year I plastered a smile on my face, tied on an apron and got down to making it the best I possibly could. I usually held it together until it was the time he unwrapped whatever gift I had got for him and every year, without fail, my heart would break. Seeing his face light up with joy and wondering if this was the last time I would see it floored me. Trying to be happy when all you want to do is hide is the worst feeling in the world. I still find Christmas unbearably hard.

Hope became my enemy: if all I had left was hope, then I was at a very low ebb. We had plenty of other avenues to go down before all we had was pitiful, measly, 'end of the road' hope. Little did I realise that hope, towards David's end, was my closest ally. Hope was to become a thing of beauty to me.

Chapter Seven
HOSPITALS

Once the radiotherapy was complete and we had learned to cope with David's diagnosis, we went into a holding pattern of hospitalisations, treatments, therapists, and medication reviews. We were offered six-monthly scans for tumour changes but soon changed to yearly scans, which helped us get on with as normal a life as possible in the interim. We found that most people would wish us luck and be incredibly supportive for a scan appointment but they didn't quite understand (through no fault of their own obviously) that the scan meant nothing to us, it was a box to be ticked; but waiting for results was emotionally draining: will we get a call the next day? Will we hear in a week? Is no news good news or has someone forgotten to call? And the follow up with family: *No, not heard anything yet. Yes, I am sure we will. No, we aren't worried. Yes, we are fine.* It all took its toll. Over time we learned that David's clinical signs and symptoms changed so quickly it seemed highly unlikely that a change in tumour would occur just when the scan was due. So we stopped the scans. We picked our battles.

I learned that within a day David could go from being fit, to being on the edge of life. There was no time for emotion, no time for panic, no time for me to feel my own fear. David needed me and I wouldn't fail him. I got him safe; I kept him warm, hydrated, pain-free. I administered his rescue medication, took pulses, temperatures, blood pressures, I monitored his eyes, and his breathing. I made the call. I kept him alive. The responsibility of that is immense, especially when we had our son in a room next door. Invariably David took a turn for the worse at night, probably because of the strains of the day. I learned there is a relief that comes with letting others take on the burden of care of a loved one. My sleep was heavier, over the years to come my recuperation was often coupled with David's hospital stays.

David had four major hospitalisations in the space of three years, between 2013 and 2015, the first probably being the most traumatic as it was the most shocking and prolonged. David had excruciating abdominal pain and we had no idea what it was. He was admitted to hospital via A&E and then onto the Medical Assessment Unit, where scans revealed that David had appendicitis – how unlucky can you get?! He was operated on and released the next day. However, his pain worsened, and, in addition, his cognitive function decreased, he went into quite a rapid decline which caused re-admittance and another operation where three drains were inserted. He was on a ward at the time, but he wasn't eating or drinking. His short-term memory deteriorated, and he became quite confused, shouting at the ward staff one night and trying to pull out his tubes. I had explained to them how David's short-term memory was not good and to call me, no matter what the time, so that I could speak to him, but they didn't (I think they were being kind and trying to give me time to sleep). This led to him being transferred to a side room and I was then allowed to stay with him if the paediatric wards were not using their truckle bed and were happy to loan it to me. So, I would wait until about 10pm to hear whether there was a bed and, if yes, I would lie next to him in the room waiting for sleep to come. David woke frequently and would wake me and we would talk through what lines were attached to him, me having photos on my phone so he could see the central line coming out of his neck.

David then contracted *clostridium difficile*, a particularly nasty infection causing diarrhoea. This led him to be isolated. David was losing a lot of weight and he needed another operation as his pain was still bad and a scan had shown more internal bleeding. David now had a nasogastric tube, central line and six drains. He was being fed parentally and we were discussing moving him to intensive care. Due to the bleeding and lack of stabilisation his epilepsy was becoming uncontrolled, and I was at a point when I couldn't leave him. So, I set up my office in the hospital room and worked from there. We managed to get him home three weeks after the initial surgery and I left for Singapore with work. My parents had George during this time and also Brandy, our dog, so they also had David whilst I was away – for the period of five days. One day out, three days of meetings, one day home. On the second day I was in Singapore I got a call from home to say that David had been readmitted. I couldn't get home early so flew as planned and drove straight from Heathrow to the hospital. He was taken to theatre about an hour after I got to the hospital. More internal bleeding, more drains. I set up my office in with David again and he was in absolute agony. I distinctly remember asking the nursing team to page a consultant as it was the weekend. When the consultant arrived, it was the closest time I have ever come to completely losing my temper. After he had finished reassuring me that David had had all the pain relief that he could I remember asking him whether he would like to see one of his family members in this much pain. David was then prescribed an intramuscular pain killer to try and break the back of the pain. I learned never to back down, to go with my gut, to be David's advocate.

This was the only time I ever witnessed David losing his faith. He did not understand how things could be so bad and why God had let this happen to him. I flew out of the room and called our vicar, a family friend who had married us, who I announced my pregnancy to and later baptised George. He came straight away. When I went back to David's room there was a new nurse present. We hadn't met him before and he was talking calmly to David, relaxing him. I told David that our vicar was on his way. The nurse explained that he was also a Christian and proceeded to tell David about his faith and beliefs. I could see David visibly relax and calmed by the nurse's quiet strength. When our vicar arrived, we did a quiet healing service with oils to anoint David's ravaged body. By this stage he was skin and bone and you could see every single vertebra of his spine. David was due to have several drains out and he was so scared as the first three that were removed were so painful, so the nurse promised to do them for him. The next day, true to his word, he came and removed the drains without any pain at all. It was simply amazing to see and this nurse, to me, was a miracle, sent when we needed him.

Once David was clear of the *clostridium difficile* infection he was moved back onto the ward, but he continued to lose weight. His bowel then went into ileus, which basically means it stopped functioning properly. Something that we would see several times with David. Over the course of several days the nursing team and I tried everything to get it going again but to no avail. We resorted to a suppository, and one was inserted. However, the shock then sent David into a grand mal seizure and we had to fast-page the team to help bring him round and make sure that he was able to go to the toilet if he needed to. This was a very low point for us both as David looked so ill and his cognitive function had deteriorated. However, we managed to bring him round in time.

We then started on the road to recovery which was a long and painful process. David had been in hospital for well over a month and had become institutionalised. He felt safe in the hospital and didn't want to leave but I was torn between being with David, being at home, being with George and working. I was exhausted when I left the hospital at night, and I just needed to sleep. My parents had George, I knew he was safe, and I occasionally took him to see David, but he had only just turned two years and David didn't like George to see him in hospital. I remember once sitting on the edge of my seat as George climbed in and out of the hospital bed mechanism. Holding tightly to the controls in case David accidently lowered himself and George got something trapped. But I was too exhausted to stop George. David had also become quite demanding:

he wanted this t-shirt because it was thinner than that one, not the hoodie as he couldn't lie back in bed properly, these shorts were too thick, not tracksuit bottoms as they wrapped round his legs….and the list went on. But part of me welcomed the 'picky-ness' for if he was being picky, he was still interested in life, he still had an opinion, and he wasn't being apathetic. Every day I would arrive, get him out of bed, washed and showered and change his sheets. He didn't like/wouldn't eat the hospital food (there was nothing wrong with it, I used to eat it instead and often it was the only food I got a chance to eat so; waste not: want not!) or the supplement milkshakes so I popped into M&S and got smoked salmon appetisers, fresh fruit, chocolates – whatever we could to tempt him to eat. The ward staff let me store our food in their fridge as everyone was concerned about his weight. Slowly David stabilised but his bloods remained stubbornly non-cooperative. David had low sodium, much lower than the normal range and enough to cause most concern. Mostly due to his epilepsy medication but he could function at his normal level. As the sodium levels weren't moving, we decided we needed to start getting David home. I was becoming more and more exhausted with the juggling and George needed some home time. The ward staff could see I was starting to suffer, and they told me I was making life too easy for David to stay. So, we decided that David would come out on day release and we would try a few nights at home. The days went well and then came the night. I picked David up and brought him home, settled him on the settee and then went for a glass of wine. No sooner than I sat down the phone rang, it was the hospital: Was David OK? His sodium levels had dropped further, was he conscious? David was fine, but he had heard the conversation and wanted to go back to hospital. It was the last straw and I finally flipped, I belted back to hospital and more or less rolled him out of the passenger seat telling him to find his own way back to the ward. It wasn't my finest moment, but would it happen the same way again? Probably.

David eventually came home a few days later when the sodium level monitoring showed no change. We learned to live with it. His sodium levels would continue to haunt us and I pray for the day when all test results are stored centrally. The whole episode was about two months long and left our whole family exhausted.

In the spring of 2014, we decided to have a party in the back garden with a hog roast and bouncy castle for the kids. My parents helped with the arrangements as David's function wasn't brilliant still. He spent a lot of time sitting on the settee or sleeping. It was quite frustrating, but he was doing the best he could. He really excelled himself at the party and joined in with everything. However, the next day he couldn't move out of bed, all his extremities were white and freezing cold, he couldn't talk and he was shaking with cold. We wrapped him up in as many blankets as we could find and George helped feed Daddy off a spoon. I also remember asking George to find Daddy a hat and he went and got his Spurs cap; it was so sweet. He just sat with David and cuddled him. David continued to decline and the visiting doctor called an ambulance. The paramedics recommended that we take him in so he was taken by ambulance to hospital. My parents came to sit with George and I went with the ambulance. By the time we arrived David was unable to talk but was still conscious, he just couldn't get the words. I was taken into the resuscitation unit with him as I was the only one that could say what had happened. David had abdominal bloods taken as they couldn't get blood from anywhere else. He was stabilised again and admitted. On this occasion David was put on a drip for twenty-four hours and he was more of less back to normal. I started to learn that if David's brain didn't get what it needed it just took from the rest of David's body. Once his brain was happy again then his body was permitted to be. David's clinical signs and symptoms were a real yardstick by which we started to measure his overall health. We stopped looking for the 'normal' signs of tumour activity and looked at how David was.

As a couple we were so very fortunate. Our medical team remained consistent and communication was amazing. We had a couple of wonderful GPs who knew us well, David's neurologist and oncologist were superstars and our hospice team were phenomenal.

We were active participants in David's healthcare plan and our opinions were listened to and sought and acted upon. It helped us understand that we could have some control over what was happening to us.

The next episode, in late 2014 was slightly more serious. Sometime later David was getting increased breakthrough focal seizures and auras so after seeing our amazing neurologist, Dr. Tim Harrower, David was introduced to a new anti-epilepsy medication. The letter was written up and sent to our GP who subsequently prescribed the medication. Epilepsy medication must be carefully managed: you slowly titre (increase) and taper (decrease) so that the brain has time to accept and adjust to the medication. David started the new medication with no problems and we were following the titre programme that had been sent to us. A couple of weeks in, David started to get headaches and see double, and he also started vomiting heavily. Again, an ambulance was called and, this time, we were blue lighted to Exeter. Following an ambulance in a car is no fun, especially going through red lights and roadworks but the ambulance crew had told me to stay behind them so I did, white knuckled and gripping the steering wheel tightly. I parked and went into A&E to see David more or less unconscious in the bed. David was taken directly onto a side room on a ward and I kept telling the staff that he needed to take his medication as otherwise his epilepsy wasn't going to be controlled. So, he was given more medication. I left for the night once he was settled, there was nothing else I could do.

The next day I returned to hospital and David appeared a little brighter, asking if he had had his medication, he said no but they were doing the round. The doctors duly came in to see us and explained that there had been a mistake made. Our GP had misread the medication dosage that David was due to have of the new medication that had led to him having twice as much as he should have. Once David came off the medication and was decreased to what he was meant to be having he returned to normal again and he came home a couple of days later. This really taught us to respect and understand our doctors and medical teams. We expect them to know everything and to be almost superhuman, but they are just people like us, trying to make the right decisions to get the best outcome, working under extreme pressure and long hours. In the majority of jobs, when you make a mistake you can apologise and put it right. When a physician makes a mistake, it can sometimes be the difference between life and death. But it doesn't change from the fact that it is still a mistake and no-one makes a mistake on purpose. It is incredibly unlikely that a doctor prescribes a double dose of medication on purpose. There is absolutely nothing wrong with treating everyone with compassion and understanding and I know that our (fabulous) GP would have beaten themselves up more than any words from us would have done. Forgiveness and understanding cost nothing. It is all about love.

Our last trip to hospital in 2015 was a pivotal moment in David's illness. David had been out chopping logs with Dad as I'd asked Dad to help me get David active. He was increasingly drawing into himself, communicating less and I needed to get him engaging with life and activity. It was late 2014 and George was now three and needed his father. So, Dad came along and the pair of them chopped and stacked wood ready for the winter. However, the next day David had headaches and started to have blurred vision. By the evening I tried to get him up to dance with me to Moon River (it was our anniversary and Moon River was our first dance) but he couldn't stand. At the table at dinner, he couldn't hold his cutlery and so ate with his hands. George couldn't understand what was happening, and neither could I. The next day David was completely out of it, he couldn't find his mouth with food, or drink. I sat him outside and called a paramedic friend who sat with him whilst we waited for the ambulance to come. David was taken to Exeter again, I followed in the car.

When we got to hospital it was clear that the staff were worried. David had very little speech, no recall and little movement. There were concerned looks and discussion of a stroke. I was hanging over David's bed trying not to cry and telling him that I would be there and that we would get speech therapists and whatever was needed to make him right. He just needed to hang on and concentrate on getting better. I told him I loved him over and over again, holding his lifeless hand, looking into his trapped eyes. But then I had a revelation, my concern and solicitude were only making this more alarming for him. Our normal *modus operandi* was that David would lie in bed sleeping and I would tap away on my laptop answering emails and basically just cracking on with life until we got some news. So that's what I did, I went back to the car, retrieved my laptop, and started to work. And I could see David visibly relax as, if I was not worried, then he had no cause to. David was admitted to the high dependency unit and I went home. The next day I returned to Exeter; I remember it was a Friday. George was at nursery, my parents again wading into the breach, and sat with David in the HDU when Tim Harrower, David's neurologist, came to see me and we went into a side room for a chat. He explained that David had had a brain bleed and if he were to have another seizure over the weekend he might not make it. We had previously discussed our expression of wishes and I reaffirmed that David did not want to be resuscitated if he lost further cognitive function or would not be himself. David's oncology nurse was called and we updated his 'red form'. It was told that this would be a good time to call family. I made the call.

The DNR form, or the red form, is a piece of paper that accompanies a person wherever they go when they are end of life. There are questions on there that you didn't know you would ever need to answer. Knowing David's wishes didn't make taking the final decision any easier and I left the hospital that night feeling my heart was being torn apart and wondering whether he *truly* meant what he said…and now we were there, would he *really* want that? But those doubts are healthy doubts and I suppose was helping me come to terms with what could happen.

Chapter Eight
IN YOUR HANDS

On the way home from the hospital, I felt the need to go to church. All Saints Church in North Molton was about a fifteen-minute drive further on from our house and was on the way to my parents. By the time I arrived, I resembled a squashed tomato, I have never been able to cry like they do in films…it's just not a pretty look. As I arrived at the church, the choir had just finished practicing and one of them saw me and came over to give me a hug. Hugs are one of God's great joys and I'll never stop appreciating the love and comfort that can be provided through someone else's touch. It is my go-to when I see people in pain. The person offered to accompany me into the church and I remember kneeling in the front pew on the left-hand side. I just prayed…and prayed. I went up to the high alter and kneeled against the alter rail and clearly remember saying to God: I place my family into your hands. I trust you.

And then there was a peace, a peace inside me knowing that I didn't need to struggle or fight anymore, that He would do what was right for us and I put every grain of trust I had in Him. If I were to lose David, then this was the right time for us. George knew his father and, a few years ago, that was all we wished for.

To this day I will see what happened as a miracle: three days later David came home. Until the time of his progression, he never had another seizure and cognitively he was the best he had been for years. That was September 2014.

Chapter Nine
DAVID

After David came home from hospital we entered a time of quiet joyfulness. His medication was stable, he was active and was enjoying life again. I think it had given us all a bit of a scare and made us appreciate life more. David wasn't quite the same but he was happy and smiling and that's all I wanted. There is a beauty in relaxing and finding peace in daily routine, of looking at life as a simple pattern which repeats and that definitely appealed to David. We had another year where we were and then our dream house came on the market and we moved to North Molton, the village where we got married and had George baptised. We overlooked the church that I had gone to pray that fateful evening. David was seizure free and amazingly got his driving licence back. He drove locally, going to the market, shopping, walks on the moor and taking George to sports and various clubs. David loved walking George down to the local school and chatting with the parents at the gate. David's was a peaceful life and had little complexity and that's just what he needed.

David's days were trouble free. He took his time over absolutely everything, forty-five minutes wasn't long enough to have a shower, shaving became almost a ritual and he wouldn't start anything if he had to be out of the house in an hour. He had to rev himself up to make a sandwich. He could spend a whole day with a basket of ironing and preparation for the evening meal was quite often started at lunch time. David was doing things in his David way, at his David pace. I was asked if it frustrated me, but why would it? There was very little point in him rampaging through the day and then getting bored. This slow pace suited us all and I loved him for it. George always had perfectly turned-out school uniform, dinner was on the table most evenings (although sometimes it was a little strange, we had chilli one day but David had forgotten the kidney beans and put curry powder in instead of chilli) but overall, we had no complaints. If I needed him to do something I would start asking him several weeks in advance of it needing to be done and we would get there in the end. I can remember a male friend laughingly telling me that 'this was just blokes'. But the point was missed: this wasn't my 'bloke', this wasn't pre-tumour David. We learned to adapt. I learned to accept the new normal.

I remember reading once about how to live and accept people who had suffered a brain injury and it was a revelation to me. I had never seen David as a person suffering brain trauma, but that is what it was, his poor brain, over the years, had been traumatised time and time again. No wonder he needed to go gently. David was the most mindful person I know, living in the moment, living for the moment.

David was relatively healthy for a period over five years and during that time our relationship changed beyond recognition. Over time David did less and I did more. David started to become more childlike, and I started to show him the same patience as I would a child (sometimes not a lot then!) Things started to become slower, a little more frustration from him showed. But the change was so gradual, such a slow, insidious creep that we barely noticed. On reflection, probably like his brain tumour. It took him longer to sort his medication, he got days mixed up, he forgot things, names and addresses were challenging for him. On the rare occasions we would go out together I started to save conversations so I could gently steer the conversation for him. But they were all harmless things that we didn't clock as anything more sinister.

David didn't like to talk about his cancer, but he did go to the local hospice to the patient group once a week at various times over the years. David and his hospice driver became very close over the period of time and, as David's father had died, it was a relationship that was particularly dear to him. He was able to talk to someone, with no judgement, outside of our support circle. For David, having that opportunity was really important to him and I welcomed the relationship. It didn't really worry me that he might be saying something to another person that I might not like, the most important thing is that he had someone there. I had some work colleagues who were the same to me and I feel that opportunity to discuss things, one step removed from your family and friends, who is not necessarily a professional, can be very helpful as all those things that you think of in the dark of the night can be tentatively explored and held gently. The hospice was a wonderful support to us all and we took part in a number of fundraisers for them as well as helping out on others. As David was able to help the hospice in return for them helping us, I felt it helped him feel useful in the world.

Physically, David still looked healthy, apart from the weight gain and his wonky head, he hadn't changed visibly. He was always smiling, dispensing hugs and laughter with a Northern Irish accent. He loved saying 'elephant poo' instead of 'I love you' (try lip reading 'elephant poo' in a mirror – it looks like you are saying 'I love you'). He would save all his energy for when he went out of the house, he wouldn't really acknowledge the tumour in any way. But when he got home, he was so tired that he often needed to rest. I found this difficult to deal with as it gave everyone a false impression of what our life was like. But it also gave me real insight and understanding of what the expression: 'what goes on behind closed doors' means.

David could put on an amazing display for outside. A particular example of this was that David used to cook lunches for the village luncheon club. He did it a couple of times with a friend and I always encouraged him to take part. However, when he said he was cooking, inside I knew the onus of preparation and getting him to where he needed to be was going to fall on me. It seems selfish and churlish to say that but on top of my life, it nearly brought me to tears. David wanted to do thing himself and he would spend hours looking at recipes, but he struggled with following the steps and couldn't retain the information between reading it and doing it. This obviously was a source of frustration to him so it was a fine line for me to walk; letting him do the cooking and preparation, but making sure he had the right things, in the right amount, at the right time, and at the right temperature. Things that come naturally to most were difficult for him. So, I used to help him get everything done quietly behind the scenes and usher him out of the door with his food and clear instructions on how he needed to 'finish off' the dish. Then I would clear up the carnage in the kitchen and play catch up with work for the rest of the day. David was absolutely delighted when people liked what he'd cooked; he loved the praise and validation it brought him. Who was I to take that away?

Much of the time David kept a smile on his face and had a sunny and happy outlook on life. Since that one time in hospital, he hadn't had any serious wobbles that I could remember. But once, I recall coming back from church group on a Friday evening. He'd found life particularly difficult for a few weeks and he just lay there quietly and told me that he thought he would be better off dead. I realised then, that as much as I wished it to be 'over' sometimes, I still wanted to be able to make the decision and to own the call. I went into over-drive; there was no need for that, there was no way he would be better off dead; we loved him and he was needed. He was the first person in our family of three. I poured all my strength and love into that conversation which was made all the more forceful because he was voicing some of the emotions that I knew I had been feeling. We talked for hours, we laughed, we cried, and we told each other how we couldn't live without the other. He never told me he wanted it to be over again.

.

Chapter Ten
COPING

Coping is a funny thing; you sort of don't know you aren't until the wheels come off. I lost count of how many people said that I was coping well, that I was strong, and that I was an inspiration. However well-meaning those statements were and how the person meant them kindly and with love, compassion, and admiration – a statement of encouragement, I could just feel myself either dying inside or (which was more frequent towards the end) getting quite aerated. What choice did I have? Did they think I wanted to be strong? No, I wanted to curl into a ball and cry, I wanted to stop the world and get off. But that choice was not open to me. I had a husband who was ill and a child who needed to see life as normal as it could possibly be. I lived my life spinning plates, juggling balls, and keeping a smile on my face. Doing was so much easier than being. There was an occasional yearning to be mindful and alone with my thoughts, but in reality that was too scary. However, sometimes everything fell down around me.

I remember one morning driving into our local town with David in the car, it must have been a weekend and it was when George was young. I don't remember what had happened or why I was so upset but I just remember hitting the steering wheel with both hands, really whacking it so that my hands hurt and the steering wheel shook.

Grabbing it until my knuckles were white. I was shouting at David that I needed help, that I needed him to help me, that I couldn't cope anymore. I was hard, uncompromising, pouring out all my pent-up emotion and stress. I looked at David sitting in the passenger seat, staring out of the windscreen, totally lost, bewildered. He genuinely didn't know how to act or what to say – and my heart broke all over again. For him, for me, for our son. For the life we could never, ever have again. I think it was at that point that I truly realised I was on my own, the only person that was going to save me was me. From that day on I rarely lost it in front of David again, I rarely let the wheels come off. It wasn't fair on him; he never meant any harm; he was doing his best.

So, my coping mechanism started to include my parents. I consider myself to be blessed with my parents. My Dad considers himself to be my own personal life coach and my Mum is a constant presence of love and understanding. As much as I tried to shelter them from really seeing how difficult I was finding things, sometimes I just needed to vent. On occasion I would take myself off to their house and shout and swear; railing against God, the unfairness of life, how this was my life too that was getting messed up. Using every expletive I could find and feeling that a cathartic stream of abuse would somehow make me feel better, but it just left me drained and even more depleted than before. But that in itself was good, because there is only one way to go when you hit rock bottom.

I always had a sense of regret and worry when I left my parents, although it gave me the strength to carry on, I felt that I had off loaded my pain to them. I would receive messages and emails from my Mum at all hours, long ones, telling me that they loved me, they were proud of me and they were there for me. Whilst I had crashed to sleep, my parents had probably sat up talking, trying to make sense and lay plans for a situation where there was no sense to be made, where no plans could be laid.

I think it is important here to say how important my Mum was to me. I am fortunate in that I have someone in my life who loves me completely and unconditionally. I am ashamed to say that, in my darkest moments I took advantage of that. I lashed her with my tongue and my razor-sharp wit. I knew where the chinks in her armour were and I knew what would get to her. I suppose subconsciously I think I wanted her to hurt as much as I was hurting. My Mum took all of this without complaint or bitterness; psychologically accepting my burden. She was never resentful, rarely upset and always loving. My mother is under five foot tall but this diminutive woman had more strength than me, by a long stretch. Mum was steadfast and remained strong, never faltered under the weight of my hurt, anger, and grief. My Mum knows me better than myself, whilst I have told her I'm sorry for my actions, she brushes it aside and tells me she knows. I love my Mum and have the utmost respect for her.

I frequently reference coping to being like a Weeble, the 1970s egg-shaped toys with the round heavy bottom (not unlike myself now I mention it!) When you knock them, they rock to one side and then the balance of weight causes them to right themselves and wobble before becoming stationary, fully righted. I frequently referred to myself as a Weeble. We would get bad news, it would totally floor us, we'd be down for a couple of days and then very, very slowly we would start to bob back to our upright position; wobble a bit at the top and then stand straight, accepting the new normal. Over time we came to recognise the pattern of coping and it became quite a routine for us. Hear something, make all the necessary calls, give ourselves a couple of days to process, then slowly bounce back. This became such an important coping mechanism for us that a good friend bought me an original Weeble – and it sits on my chest of drawers with all my other loved possessions. In my head, I would like to consider myself to be like a willow on the edge of a river, bending gracefully when the winds grow stronger, allowing the winds to blow through the leaves but after the wind has blown itself out, returning to her upright position, with a few leaves missing but with the same graceful presence. Then my brain asserts itself, who am I kidding, I am that heavy-bottomed toy!

I learned, over time, to accept what people said with equanimity. A good proportion of people don't know what to say or how to act. When you are living with something on a daily basis you get accustomed to the tiny changes, the new normal. When you are confronted suddenly with someone who is ill, people just panic and don't know what to do or say. I found it easier to help people by just agreeing with what they said: *Doesn't David look amazingly well? Yes he does. Are you coping well? Yes we are. You wouldn't know he was ill would you? No, you wouldn't.* All said with a smile on my face. There is no harm in helping people express their solidarity with you and there is very little mileage and even less satisfaction in actually being honest and reply with: *He might look well but actually we're all dying a little bit more every day. No, frankly we aren't coping a lot of the time but we are muddling through. Yes, you would actually know he was very ill if you knew how he was before.* I always have been and always will be a glass half full person and I was always aware that if you were too open or negative then people will stop asking or talking about it. Having friendly and well-meaning enquiries is so much better than no caring questions at all and if you say things with enough conviction and confidence you can even start to believe them yourself.

So, my brave face became a kind of permanent make-up, something I put on when facing the 'real world', something that didn't allow anyone to see what was happening below the surface. I very rarely said that I wasn't coping and that I needed help…and when I did say that I wasn't coping I had really got past the point of being able to be helped easily. Over the years I learned what my triggers were for indicating that I wasn't coping and was able to take the right steps to try and help myself, and my family, before my grief and anger became too destructive.

I've mentioned previously about how grief and anger can be destructive and sometimes the recognition of the destructive nature can happen a bit too late. I look back on the person I was before, the person I was in the middle, the person I am now, and have to hold them all quite gently. David's illness meant that a lot of the situations I had to deal with, I did it alone. It's quite a difficult place to be and I am full of admiration for single-parent families. I had, and still have, three destructive tendencies: alcohol, spending and working. My personality, without going into too much psychology is very driven and I'm very: 'in for a penny in for a pound'. I found all my destructive habits spiralled in times of severe stress…I would start to, for example, enjoy a drink and relax, perhaps in front of my computer in the evening. Before I knew it, I was drinking a bottle of wine a night and chained to my desk. I drank to forget and to relax and I worked because I knew that one day I would probably need to use the brownie points I accrued. I always wanted the best for David and George and, as I was usually unable to give them time, I spent money on them…a lot of money. Always trying to give them the best that I could, I really don't know why. Was it an attempt to make things look normal, trying to make up for spreading myself too thinly amongst all my other responsibilities. Who can say?

One thing that I never got used to was the change in David's and my physical relationship. I am a hugging and kissing type of person and I see a physical relationship with your partner as an extension of that. I love that feeling of *really* being held, of your souls meeting when you look into someone's eyes. Conveying a meaning with just a touch on your arm, the small of your back, a light kiss on your neck. My most favourite thing is when you are truly being held in another person's arms, your hands holding the other person; not just touching, naked flesh caressing naked flesh almost so your bodies meld together. I lost that the day that George was born as I catapulted from wife and confidant to mother and carer. I mourned the loss of our intimacy, but David no longer understood what was appropriate and I didn't have the strength to teach him. As David's illness progressed something changed in my head, he was like a child and it was totally wrong to have an intimate relationship with a child. I saw a counsellor about it, George must have been about six at the time, and she asked me what was stopping me and encouraged me to push my boundaries. That night I remember climbing into bed, no clothes on, asking David to hold me, telling him I just wanted to lie with him. I lay there, stiff as a board and then slowly relaxed so we could cuddle each other. But in the cold light of day the barriers went back up and I couldn't bring myself to repeat it. I decided to put that part of our relationship away. We always maintained a close and loving relationship with lots of cuddles and kisses, but never ever intimate. I never passed the mark of what I would have found acceptable to do with my son, after all, you are not intimate with a child.

I had a couple friends that have been with me since (more or less) day one. They saw me through the worst times and they always had the ability to put things into perspective. But not only that, they did something even more important, they took their cues from me and followed my emotional journey. If I wanted to rant with indignation, they ranted with me, if I cried, they held me when I cried, if I needed to rail against the injustice of life, they did that with me, if I wanted to be told that sex wasn't worth it by the end of the conversation we were all ready to be nuns! If I laughed but inside was dying, they laughed with me; seeing my pain but allowing me to express myself in the way that I needed to. They only ever put me right when I asked for it, they listened, helped, cared, were never judgemental when I overstepped or got it wrong. They kept my confidences. They were David's friends just as much, but I knew they were first and foremost in my camp, 100% on my side; they always had my back. They will always be my gift and I couldn't have got through it without them. Everyone in life needs those friends, those that stick by you through thick and thin. I remember my parents telling me that you can count your true friends on one hand and having been through hell and back again, I can categorically state that I believe that to be true. Your souls and minds will choose each other. Eugene Peterson wrote 'Writing cheerful graffiti on the rocks in the valley of deep shadows is no substitute for companionship with the person who must walk through the darkness'[1]. Louisa and Tash, thank you from the bottom of my heart.

[1] *Peterson, E., 1996, 'Five 'Smooth Stones for Pastoral Work' page William B Eerdmans Publishing Company, p136.*

One very surreal aspect was something that our family came to know as 'the adrenaline bubble' and I really do thank God for the wonderful ways that human body behaves when under severe stress. Over the years we got into quite a routine when David was ill. The initial flurry of activity that ensued after David was admitted to hospital, for one of a variety of reasons, soon became a logistical nightmare of school runs, hospital visits, work meetings and updating people with how David was doing. It is amazing how much you can cram into a day when you need to. These periods of intense pressure ran from three days to eight weeks. However, on every single occasion, two or three days after David was home we forgot what had really happened and we slotted back into normal life with ease. Putting it behind us and not really thinking of it again. We called it the bubble as from the moment the problems started to the end, it was almost as if you were living outside of your own body and watching from a completely dissociated position. It really helped me to look at things objectively and not take rash decisions.

Coping is a funny concept, one that is not easy, and I have learned that everyone has their own ways of getting through trauma which I don't think will come as a surprise to anyone. But I would go out on a limb and assert that most people living with life limiting illness affecting friends and family will, at one or more points, not cope or cope badly. If I could offer any advice, it would be to go gently with yourself and with others in the same situation as you. Really listen, accepting 'I'm fine' is ok, but look if the person actually wants to open up as 'I'm fine' rarely means the person is…and I usually found the more people insist that they are fine, the worse they actually are. 'I'm absolutely fine' used to mean that I was about to explode. However, if someone asked me how I was and my reply was: 'Do you know what, I'm actually doing ok', I was in a very different place.

The other aspect that was important to both David and I as part of our coping mechanisms was our faith and I firmly believe that faith helps; whatever faith you might have.

.

Chapter Eleven
KEEPING FAITH

David and I enjoyed being an active part of our local church, where he is now buried. He was part of the Open the Book team, visiting local schools, which he loved as he got to dress up and have fun. We had a set of keys for the church and David unlocked and locked the church at dawn and dusk weekdays during term times, sharing the responsibility with one of the churchwardens. He loved the routine it involved and it gave his day structure. I would love to say he had a 100% track record but as his disease progressed his forgetfulness increased, but no harm ever became the church. David would also change the alter cloths and set up church for the Wednesday morning communion. Our vicar at this time was also called David and he was so gentle with him, letting him work at his own speed, not worrying if the wrong colour was out, knowing that David was working to the best of his ability.

I think these times in the church helped David keep his faith throughout his illness. When he got ill, he told me he knew where he was going and that was such a source of comfort to us both. We both believe that when you go to heaven all your earthly cares and troubles will go and so we knew that David, in heaven, would be out of pain and restored.

Penny, a wonderful friend, and vicar within our mission

community, invited us to join a church group called TGI and we got together on a Friday evening for pizza, beers, and fellowship. David and I both loved it for different reasons. At TGI David was accepted, could be himself, was under no pressure, and no judgement. We were both welcomed with open arms and love. Friday evenings were amazing, special, relaxing, restorative. Penny unerringly knew what we needed and ministered to all our needs.

My mother-in-law also had a strong faith and, right at the start of David's illness she said she would pray for a miracle; to which I tersely replied that God wouldn't send a miracle, but he might send a drug. Being in clinical research, I couldn't help but pin my hopes on medicine. When I was having my confirmation classes shortly after we were married, I remember saying to the vicar at the time, that he would never be able to make me believe in miracles. His response was that he knew a heart surgeon who had said that sometimes, on the operating table, things happened that there was absolutely no earthly explanation for. Our vicar described miracles as that; when there simply is no explanation for the wonder that has just happened. And I grew to believe that miracles do occur: when I placed my family in His hands; the fact that I fell pregnant a week before David's first seizure; and David's graceful and peaceful death were, to me, all miracles in their own right.

.

Chapter Twelve
GEORGE

I have thought many times about whether, if we knew what we were facing, would we have wanted to bring a child into this environment and heartache. As George was conceived so close to all the trauma that we had, I can only believe that he was meant to be. I know I am making sweeping statements, but I think that worry, guilt, and anxiety are emotions that are a constant presence for most mothers and I was no different. I still worry about all the stress hormones that George was exposed to when I was pregnant. I worry about the first three or four years when I was away from him for weeks at a time. I worry about giving him too many material things and not enough emotional 'me only' time. However, I have come to realise that I too, as capable as I am in my job, am just another person trying to make the right decisions in the face of something that has traumatised us both. It is only with hindsight that I realise how much David has affected us both and I need to be gentle with both myself and George. That, in turn, makes me worry that I am being too lenient on him!

George was an extremely easy baby and slept through the night at an early age. He was a happy baby and a wonderful toddler. We really felt blessed. At one point we just wanted George to be able to remember anything about his father and for David to get to see his child, but we were getting years that we didn't believe that we would. We were lucky.

But George learned things that no child should ever need to know. At four I was standing him in front of David gently telling him that this is what Daddy having a seizure looked like and that he shouldn't be alarmed if Daddy can't speak to him; he learned how to call for help and dial an ambulance. Before he was five he knew how to administer David's rescue medication and he also knew he had to keep the location of the medication secret because it could be dangerous in someone else's hands. At six, we were explaining what an MRI scanner was and what a brain tumour looked like. At seven we took him to see David's neurologist, Tim Harrower where Tim explained what happens during examinations and showed George David's tumour on his scans. At nine we realised George was starting to struggle so got him a puppy, Trampus; something to focus his love on and give him something to cuddle and bond with; in the same way Brandy was a source of comfort to me.

David and I always talked openly to George about David's tumour and the fact that Daddy would be going to heaven. We naively believed that George would be able to process the information in the same way that we could. When George was about nine years we went through some challenging times and I believe that many people with children experiencing trauma also go through. Having spoken to professionals about this, it was felt that George's challenges were coming from the transition of *knowing* that David had cancer to *understanding* what that means. Unfortunately, the time that George was starting to comprehend what was happening was the same time that David, although stable, started to deteriorate. It was not an easy time for our family but we were supported throughout by the relevant teams and, with hindsight, and I don't think we made too many mistakes.

After David died, George and I had several conversations about things that happened when David was alive. George had some regrets. A child of twelve shouldn't have regrets. George has had to grow up too quickly. But George's predominant memories of David are good and one of the best is that David used to walk passed George's bedroom door every night and tell him that he loved him. We can only support our children through these conversations and give them the tools that they need to be able to deal with the challenges that losing a parent holds. George's resilience has grown immensely over the last couple of years and he is one of the strongest boys I know and I am so very proud of him.

.

.

Part III

The End

Chapter Thirteen
CHANGES

The length of David's illness naturally began to take a toll on the family. What was once a blessing, that long life, became on occasions a torment. Sometimes we focused on the end, needing to know that it was there, needing to know there was a light at this long tunnel…whatever form the light took. Then other times, we just wanted to cling to the 'now'; better the devil you know than face the unknown. As a family we moved into quite a surreal pattern of life, not knowing when the end was coming, knowing it was, but almost pretending it wasn't there. It was unsustainable and, at some stage, the bubble had to burst.

David slowly changed over time; it took him longer to do things and he began to get more frustrated with himself when he couldn't do what he wanted. He started to question why he was still alive but, blessedly, these episodes were few and far between and usually only happened after something particularly difficult had happened at home. But, in comparison to many of the families that I had heard of with brain tumours, we were still extremely lucky. His cognitive age was also reducing, doing things that he would have found completely alien in his pre-tumour existence. One thing that became a thing close to many of our hearts was a bee costume. Our church did summer camp each year and David was the leader of the yellow team with the theme being nature. David, as usual, left getting his outfit until the very last minute and then, the day before camp started to go to the local honey farm to see if he could find anything yellow. He came home with a young child's outfit, complete with a ruffled net skirt, wand with a bee on top and a bee deely bopper head band. He looked the part and loved wearing it.....by putting the skirt over his head he could wear it round his neck.... there is nothing more inappropriate than a grown man wearing a small child's skirt round his neck…but David saw no wrong in it and was happy to go out in public, proud as punch with his costume! After the church camp was over I suggested he recycle it but he tucked it away in a drawer with his church things…a drawer he used to go into a lot…and when he did, the bee costume came out and he popped it on and wandered around the house with it on. He loved the costume. We buried him with it.

Something also happened to David's sense of humour. It grew to be hideously inappropriate and what he thought was funny was just downright insulting! On many occasions I would squirm. I distinctly remember one time, when we were the welcoming team to church one Sunday, David opened the church door to see some people in the church entrance and he asked them if they were coming or were they going to stand there gossiping. Eek! But people knew David as David and he never seemed to cause lasting offence…. that I have been told about anyway!

David also had a lot of physiological changes that he needed to adapt to. His bladder control wasn't good so he had a bag that he wore if we were going a long way from home. He hated this bag and didn't like me to ask him about it. However, his short-term memory meant that he forgot to empty it, so his bag would overflow or he would remember when we were on the motorway and couldn't do anything about it. David always needed to do things quickly because he was like a child – we all know that when you are nappy training and a toddler says they need the toilet, it means that they need it NOW – that was David. And I couldn't always get to that place quick enough. So long journeys were always quite stressful for me as David also didn't want George to know what he had to do as he still wanted to be dignified in George's eyes. We got used to regular stops in gateways, lay-bys and we always carried bottles in the car for emergencies. David also wouldn't ask someone where the toilet was in their house so we always had to stop before we arrived anywhere and stop just after we left. Just part of the adaptions that we made.

David also found it difficult to travel and stay in unfamiliar places. He could visit family Northern Ireland because he knew the house layouts, we always stayed in the same room at Center Parcs. But if we went somewhere new, he would wake up in the night and not know where the toilet was. On one occasion this resulted in him hitting the walls in frustration and I got him to the toilet just in time. But as he sat on the toilet, his stress and anxiety levels were so high he started being sick into the bin. We didn't go away again unless we had no choice. Our lives shrunk to the walls of Blakesville, our home in North Molton, and we made Blakesville as comfortable and relaxing as we could as we rarely ventured far from our home.

As a wife, all these changes were extremely hard to see. My best friend and rock was a shell of their former selves and a person that relied on me for everything: help, guidance, support, and safety. But you can't do anything else than to adapt, to put on that brave face and tell people that you don't mind; that you are fine with watching your husband slowly dying before your eyes. But the blessing was that the changes were so slow and insidious that I didn't notice the change on a daily basis. What used to catch me was when I got glimpses of what life could have been like. Things like watching video clips of our wedding and hearing David's wedding speech floored me. We went on annual trips to Center Parcs with Louisa and her husband, Malcolm, and Elsie, who was just three weeks older than George, and seeing them seamlessly work in tandem used to knock me completely off kilter. One time I came back and started counselling because it was so bad. And Louisa always understood, was always there for me, never needing to say a word. So, I got to learn that I needed to be in my bubble and not move from it. Functioning day to day with a smile on my face even though my heart had broken into a million small pieces that I thought I would never be able to put back together again.

Strange things got to me. Louisa was in Exeter hospital for some planned treatment and I went down to see her. We spent an hour catching up and as I left, wandering out of the hospital, heading home, all of a sudden I was feeling quite panicked and unsettled, I was shaking, short of breath and could feel tears coming. I couldn't work out what was happening to me. But when I got back to the car I realised: the last time I had walked along that corridor, the evening light making the fluorescent hospital lights bright and glaring, walking passed people wearing scrubs and with stethoscopes round their necks was the time I had left David, in the same ward, lying unresponsive after having the medication overdose. I soon learned to realise that the weirdest things could blindside me at a moment's notice and that I just had to weather the storm that would inevitably pass.

Chapter Fourteen
ANOTHER TEMPEST

But, as always, one day the calm didn't come after the storm. We were in lockdown during COVID and had been in lockdown since March 2020. Lockdown for our family was in many ways good. It actually gave us some much-needed downtime for us to be together at weekends. Our church group started weekly Sunday zoom meetings where people were asked to contribute and David loved this. He spent hours collecting feathers on one walk after Rachel, a great friend from church, had spoken about collecting feathers and counting blessings, he drew pictures, coloured in rainbows, and stuck them on our windows. He wrecked some of our enamel pans bashing them with wooden spoons when the weekly clapping went on to support our hospital workers. No-one asked anything of him, fewer people asked things of me. We cooked lovely things, we planted, we played badminton in the garden. The next-door house was empty and the fence had fallen down and the person looking after the house said we could use the garden, so David spent a day putting up a tent so he could sleep outside with George. Life slowed down to David's pace.

But David was changing again. Towards the end of June his speech slowed up, and he was getting terrible headaches. But more importantly, he was not able to retain information. I was on the phone to the oncology department and David's neurologist and within a week David was sent for an MRI. Travelling around in lockdown was strange as the roads were quiet and you always felt slightly guilty that you shouldn't be out. David was scanned in a mobile unit tucked in the back of North Devon Hospital. It was a lovely sunny day and I sat outside on a plastic chair with the sun on my face appreciating a little bit of quiet, hearing the gentle chatter of the hospital staff and David's occasional laughter which never failed to bring a smile to my face.

It was no surprise when we got a request from our oncologist for a call. There were changes in the tumour and David needed to see a surgeon in Plymouth to have another craniotomy. Due to it being urgent and during COVID we couldn't go to see the same surgeon in London. You know when something happens and it doesn't feel right? Well, nothing about Plymouth felt right. The surgeon didn't feel right, the hospital didn't feel right, the pre-op didn't feel right, and the time didn't feel right. I expressed my concerns to the team in Plymouth but was reassured that this was the best course of action. It still didn't feel right. But if the choice is death or jump, you jump.

So, we prepared. Trampus went down to stay with Ian Cooper, a Dog Rehabilitation specialist, in Cornwall for a week (as he had become quite an anxious and unruly dog which is another story in itself) and my ever so wonderful cousin Tracey, came down to stay and help in the house and with George. And David and I left for Plymouth. We had to be there for about 6am and the queue of people being admitted for operations snaked down the corridor. We all stood there, the patient and their nominated person, with our masks. All standing there quietly, talking in hushed tones as the line slowly moved forward. At the entrance to the ward a nurse sat at a table admitting the patient. Patients were kissing their loved ones goodbye and then going into the ward. COVID meant that the patient had to go in by themselves and couldn't be accompanied. I knew I wasn't going to leave David. It then got to our turn: I explained that David's brain tumour meant that he didn't always understand instructions and that he would need me to help him interpret what the medical team were saying. I was allowed through.

I rarely left David alone and he never needed to fight his own battles. I don't know where this primaeval need to stay with David came from. I don't understand why I couldn't leave him in capable hands. I just knew I couldn't and that I had to be there. I can only assume it was the same feeling that you have with your child – nothing and no-one was going to take him from me. I was the one who knew him best, I would fight tooth and nail to keep him safe and give him the best chance that I could to keep him alive. If it meant twisting the truth a bit, then that is what was going to happen.

We sat in a sterile room as David prepared for his operation. I was so fortunate, if I was ok and calm, he was settled. He was in his bed which, as always, he'd offered to me first. David was so lovely like that; he was always wanting me to be ok. He knew I had a long drive home after I'd seen him post-op and so his first thought was to make sure I was rested. When the team came for him, I just kissed him goodbye and waved him off with a smile on my face saying that I would check in on him later. Waving happily, he walked off with the team and I went to sit in the car for the long, long wait that is a craniotomy.

I don't know how long I sat in that car park. I can't remember eating or drinking, and I can't remember what I did for those long hours. I can remember seeing the air ambulance come in several times and thinking about the people inside. I can remember praying. I can remember it was a beautiful day and the sun was amazing. I don't know how I knew that David was out of theatre and in recovery. But I can remember waiting at the door of the ward asking if I could see him and being told I wasn't allowed on the ward. But then one lovely nurse took pity on me and told me to wait in the corridor where David would be wheeled from recovery into the ward. So, I waited, and waited….and then waited some more. I got nervous, why wasn't he here? Why hadn't he come? But then I saw him, he was sat up, head swathed in bandages and he was smiling – he was talking, he was David. The relief, the unbelievable relief of seeing him. He was amazingly well. He was safe. We talked. I smiled. The hours of agonised waiting were forgotten. I could feel the tension that had kept my shoulders up around my ears left me, along with all my strength. As David was wheeled onto the ward I turned to go home, bereft – all the adrenaline suddenly leaving my body – leaving me shaken and raw. But in front of me was our vicar from home, David and his wife, Celia. They had come to see if I was able to cope. They had come, with no agenda but to be there for me. They held me as I stood there shell shocked with the emotion of the day. Knowing that I needed to find the strength to carry on. And they gave me their strength. They gave me unconditional love.

Everyone in their lives needs people at their side – unconditionally. I have learned that the people that are there are not always the people that you expect to be. People came into my life at the right time and some stayed and some went. Some came back again and others didn't. Some I thought would understand the trauma I was going through didn't, some people that were going through hideous times themselves were able to support me, to walk alongside. As I get older I look back and realise that I spent too long being concerned about some of the people that chose not to be an active part of my life. Even though it can be awfully painful to let people go, if you can get to the end of the day with your head held up and be able to say that you did the best you could at the time, then that is enough. The people that are there for you will understand. The people that shouldn't be in your life won't, and they will go. That is the cyclical nature of life and of nature. You can't fight it, you have limited resources left to fight, so let it be.

A couple of days after David's operation I got to speak to the medical team. I was not able to go to see him, I wasn't allowed on the ward. However, I was able to join a video call with David and the medical team (after a *lot* of pushing) where we got the histology results. David's tumour had progressed to a stage IV, glioblastoma, the most aggressive form of brain tumour that you can have. The news wasn't unexpected, but that is a diagnosis that no-one ever wants to hear. We reeled. I was even more upset because I wasn't there with him – usually we had news together, we were able to discuss things quietly after, I was able to look into his eyes, watch how he moved, see how he rested. I was able to gauge what he understood and how he was feeling. I was eighty miles away and I couldn't see that. It was killing me.

David was discharged from Plymouth quickly, after just a couple of days. It felt too soon but I wasn't going to argue as COVID meant that hospitals weren't the safest place and I wanted David back with me at home. He got home and we relaxed; we were as happy as we could be, we were together. But after a few days things weren't right again, David was very sick and his headaches were shocking. Eventually I called an ambulance and he was taken back into Barnstaple, some tests were run and it was agreed that he needed to go back to Plymouth and so was ambulance transferred. It was the best place for him, but it wasn't his best place for me. My distrust of the hospital was irrational. I knew it was. I couldn't change it. I didn't want to. I should have trusted my gut.

David continued to deteriorate in hospital. I couldn't get to him; I couldn't speak to the staff. When I did, they didn't know me, they didn't know I knew what I was talking about, they didn't listen to me. I can't tell you how important a good medical team is. I am not saying that the Plymouth team was bad, we were in COVID and the hospital was under considerable pressure, it is just that we had received exceptional care to date and this just wasn't the same. Continuity of care, of understanding the patient and their situation is so key to recovery. David and I took to messenger calling all day. I would go to bed on videocam with David next to me, I would work with the camera on him. I was there every time he said 'Clare', I took him everywhere, I was his constant presence; I watched over him. But I could see him going downhill in front of me and I couldn't do anything at the other end of a screen. The soul wrenching feeling of calling someone's name and them not responding is awful – you can't touch them, you can't shake them, you can't kiss them and plead with them to wake up. When I called, no-one answered. My heart was sore and I was scared but there was one song that I played

over and over and over; it summed up the situation perfectly: JJ
Heller's '*Missing Peace*'. I still can't listen to it without crying and being
transported back to those dark days.

I remember calling out to a nurse on one occasion when they
came into David's room pleading for someone to call me as I could
never get through to the ward. David was in terrible pain, he couldn't
go to the toilet again, and it had been days. I had had enough. I got
to speak to a senior member of the team and told them I was coming
down. I was eventually allowed to see David; it was clear he wasn't
well. He was almost yellow and he was barely conscious. We agreed
that he would have an intervention to help him go to the toilet and
I was on standby for seizures. He went to the toilet but was still very
unwell. His sodium levels were well below the normal range again
and I repeatedly told the team that this was normal for him but they
didn't listen. I then spent frantic hours calling to the local doctors,
Exeter hospital, going through letters and results, compiling
information to confirm that David's sodium levels were in fact
normal for him. Even after presenting this information, I still wasn't
able to get him to come home. I knew the place he would recover
was home. I knew he needed fresh air, lovely food, a comfy bed, his
own toilet, and a normal routine. He needed care. I decided that I
was going to take him home but the team wouldn't let me. I was told
they believed he was not in control of his own decisions and
therefore, without power of attorney I couldn't take him home.

The sense of hopelessness, of hitting a brick wall could barely be
contained. I was almost possessed. These people that didn't know
David, after I had spent over a decade nursing him, of knowing every
intimate function of his body, were telling me that they knew best.
They didn't love him as I did. I explained, complained, pleaded,
cried, escalated, phoned, and called. I presented test results, I made
plans with them, we made certain conditions: If he improved, if his
sodium increased in a couple of days then he could come home. I
spent ages with David cajoling him, trying to make him recover and
get better with the force of my will power... pouring every ounce of
strength that I had into him. David's sodium didn't get better but

David stabilised. I was allowed to take him home. I was exhausted, mentally, and physically battered, but I had won, he was home.

One of the first things I did was book a meeting with our solicitor and as soon as David could get out we went and organised Powers of Attorney. A couple of months later I had them in my hand. I would never go through that again. To this day I advise everyone to get their Powers of Attorney arranged – no one needs that amount of stress in their lives, to feel that helpless.

But, as I have said before and no doubt I will say again, everything happens for a reason. The nightmare that was the hospital rather took away the nightmare that was the diagnosis. It gave us chance to get used to the diagnosis, and consequently prognosis, without really knowing we were doing it. Our bounce back was hidden underneath the umbrella of righteous indignation of unintentional imprisonment.

.

Chapter Fifteen
LIVING YOUR LIFE IN CYCLES

David started chemotherapy shortly after we got home. Again, the wheels of authority kicked into action and we had a wonderful hospice nurse assigned, David's oncologist, who had been with us since diagnosis, talked us through what needed to be done and our neurologist was there, always at the end of an email to help when we needed it. The local GP surgery, as always, was amazing and we carried on, as there was no other way, down the road that is cyclical chemotherapy regimens. The general consensus was that David would probably have another couple of years as he was fabulous at defying the odds – this was great news as it meant that David would reach his milestone of forty – after all, he had just turned thirty-nine.

We were still in the midst of COVID, locked down in rural north Devon, on the village square with the keys to the church. We were lucky. David was able to go up to the church to pray, walk the dogs round the churchyard and carry on with his life. What was previously a slow and leisurely life slowed further, again a blessing as David was slowing, but the change was swallowed up in the peace that was lockdown. We talked about what David wanted to put on his 'bucket list' and all he said he wanted was to spend time with friends and family. Simple pleasures and ones that were totally within my power to grant.

And healthcare was changing. My work was insanely busy as many clinical trials, especially in oncology, needed to continue. Getting drugs to patients, checking that they were healthy without going to hospitals and getting blood samples taken and analysed was a challenge. But it kept my mind focused and all I could think was that I needed work 'brownie points' in the bank as there was coming a time when I was going to need them. I worked tirelessly, fourteen or fifteen hours a day, interspersed with home schooling and caring for David. I often think now that my priorities were wrong and that I should have taken time to spend with my family. But I had no choice. Somewhere out there was a family like mine holding onto the hope that only medicine can bring. We all needed to pull together to make this work. Facebook became my enemy: all those families posting how precious this time with their children was – reading, doing yoga together, arts and crafts, flower pressing. It made me want to cry. I came off Facebook.

And our lives continued. On the surface it all looked perfect, but underneath was a maelstrom of emotions, of things left unsaid for the fear that once it was out there you couldn't take it back. And we were also witness to the changing face of global healthcare. David's medication was delivered to our local chemist and then delivered to our door rather than picked up from hospital or town. His blood tests were done at the GP and checked remotely by the hospital. The oncology team confirmed the next round of chemo over a video call, email replaced phone calls. Nurses came to us than us going to meet them. It was all very wonderful and convenient for us as healthcare came into our house, I barely had to leave my meetings to maintain David's treatment plan. What had previously been days out of the office and eighty-mile round trips to the hospital now were ten-minute calls. It was revolutionary. I loved it. Whilst David had always enjoyed the 'day trip' of going to the hospital to see the team, even he could see the benefit as it took a lot less out of him as he easily tired these days (and we didn't have the battle of the urine bag!)

And so, we settled into a new period of life. Our lives and calendars were marked in cycles, we planned around keeping the days before, during and after chemo free. It gave us a two-week window during which we were able to live our lives under a little less stress, a little more normality. David regressed further into himself and became even more child-like. He would go to the village shop and bring back a copy of The Times of which he then proceeded to cut out the pictures - he was meticulous at cutting along the lines. At dinner David would proudly tell George and I what was happening in each picture: a man climbing a rock, a hot air balloon, a springer spaniel. David would often get the words wrong, which we neither acknowledged nor corrected, and George would laugh and look at me as if to say, 'what is Dad on?!' and I would laugh, shrug my shoulders, and beseech him with my eyes: 'Go with it, he's happy, one day you will value these memories'. Every day I threw the pictures away or on the fire, placing the paper in the kindling basket. In the winter of 2022, I was lighting the fire one evening and at the bottom of the log basket was a copy of The Times with holes where pictures were cut out. Eighteen months after David's death. I proceeded to light the fire with the paper through my tears. I wished then I'd kept some of the pictures. I wish now I'd not used the paper to light the fire.

David loved Bear Grylls and used to say that Bear was his hero. We bought him Bear's book, '*Soul Food*', which was perfect for him to read as it was a book that contained daily spiritual readings. It used to take him hours to absorb what was written, but he loved it.

I kept a diary of episodes of headaches, blurred vision, nausea, and constipation. We would tweak and adjust steroids, codeine, and paracetamol. David was on over twenty medications a day, not counting chemotherapy and by the end of his chemotherapy we had hit over thirty different medicines. We had bought him the mother of all medicine carriers that dispensed your weekly medicine.

Every Monday morning, he would get his medicines out and spend a couple of hours sorting them into the chambers so that he knew what to take and when. I had made an excel table of what medications at what strength was needed – it was printed and laminated. He carried a version in his wallet – just in case. He loved sorting out his medicines and wouldn't let anyone else get involved. However, he was absolutely useless at remembering to take them. Four times a day he had reminders on his phone going off: firstly to tell him to take his medication, then fifteen minutes later another went asking him if he had taken his meds and then fifteen minutes later another reminder would go off saying: 'Stop everything and take your medications NOW'. And he still didn't remember. It was a source of amusement to us and, luckily, David always maintained the ability to laugh at himself.

His phone was his lifeline: he wrote down our friend's names and who was married to whom, the people that went to church, names of the people in the village shop, family members and their children...all those things that come naturally to us. He wrote down what he was grateful for, for prayers and blessings, how much spaghetti and rice is considered one portion. He made notes on his passwords, our address, his phone number, films he wanted to watch. He even wrote down what he loved me for; I found this on his phone after David died: *Thank you Lord for my wife! She it blessed with kindness, thoughtfulness, and determination with everything in her live. Clare you are amazing!* Complete with spelling mistakes – I had to love him. Some of the notes I found after he died broke my heart: *Get more confident. Why worry, who really cares! Just do it! Tasks, golf, TT, out, walk sleep. Main thing....be honest with yourself!'* and that was from January 2017. I never knew. I never fully understood his challenges.

Chapter Sixteen
THE POWER OF BEING IN A GROUP

I joined a group on Facebook called 'We are the Wives of GBM [*glioblastoma*] and this is our Story' (and of course husbands/partners were also included but as glioblastoma predominantly affects men it was mostly women). These strong women were a source of great comfort to me and the knowledge that they had was second to none; it would rival any medical team. And I didn't hesitate to ask questions. David was getting constipated but no problem; about twenty or thirty different treatments, dietary changes, 'things to try' would be given to me within the hour. And you know what…they worked! If someone wanted to question starting a new med, this amazing group of women knew the side-effects, when to take it, what to take it with, and what to look out for. When we were down, they were always there with the right words. Funny things would happen too, posts like: 'My husband has just bought a new tent, camping stove, sleeping bag etc…. he hates camping, he not camped in twenty years'. Then the responses: 'my husband's just put a deposit down on a yacht!'; 'My husband ran up $10,000 clothes shopping'…and it went on… After that post I called the bank and asked them to notify me with any unlikely spending in case I missed it! But these posts made me laugh. These women knew what hospital was running which clinical trial, which institute favoured what treatment regimen.

But it was full of heartache as well: women were being hit by their husbands, they were being verbally abused, they were being thrown out of family homes. But one thing was always the same, unfailingly: these women stood by these men that were changing beyond recognition as this hideous disease was eating away at their husband's brains. They understood, they accepted, they loved, and they never judged – not the person with the tumour, themselves, or each other. So rare on social media now.

And it made me appreciate how lucky we were. David was forgetful but he was still the laid-back David I loved; he was just buried deep inside. As the months ticked by I knew that death was around the corner and I knew the average life expectancy of a GBM patient was eight months but I also knew that many patients stayed alive for months in a critical condition: their bodies healthy, their brains fighting a war they were never going to win. I dreaded David's death. But I had my Facebook group, my lifeline, my source of truth, inspiration, compassion, and companionship.

These women, to this day, were the strongest group of people I have ever come across and I thank them for being my friends and recognise them for the strong warriors that they are.

.

Chapter Seventeen
AND THE CALM OF BEING ALONE

Christmas 2020 was another blessing for us. We were locked down so it was just the three of us. David wanted to cook Christmas Dinner which, traditionally in the UK is three courses. He wanted to cook Beef Wellington (which is not known to be easy) and he wanted to do it by himself. So, we got all the things that he needed and he started to cook. We ate four hours later than planned and were too full to eat the pudding. After we sat outside with a glass of wine and watched the sun set. He was a very happy man. Where before I would have wanted to take over, to have made it perfect, I had learned to be at rest. George was happy eating chocolate and I was happy sitting and chatting. What did it matter? Seeing the smile on his face when he carved the Wellington was worth the wait. I'd learned to not worry about the small things and find the beauty in the every day. I will always thank David for teaching me that.

But the Christmas calm was not to be maintained for long. We had postponed David's chemotherapy to allow him to have a couple of drinks over Christmas and the New Year. But into the New Year he was getting headaches and was smelling things like coffee when there was nothing around. He was also getting quite constipated and we had previously been able to manage that with the help of David's medical team and my trusty Facebook friends. I would think nothing of jumping off a meeting, slapping on a pair of gloves, popping in a suppository, and then heading back to work for ten to fifteen minutes before shouting up to David to see how he was getting on. To David, this was excruciatingly embarrassing, but for me it was just another face of what we were dealing with so we might as well just crack on! But this time nothing seemed to move. I spoke to the doctors; we were on a watching brief.

Obviously, fate being what it is, meant that George's birthday was around the corner and so, as we were still in lockdown, David had bought some buns for George and his friends. It was my job to drive round the evening before and deliver a bun per child (complete with birthday candle) to the doorsteps of the friends' houses and then we were going to do a friend zoom and a family zoom after. The buns were duly delivered but David was going downhill. At about 3am I called an ambulance: David was cramping, his hands were tingling, he was extremely nauseous and was very bloated – his stomach was like a drum. The ambulance took David to hospital at around 4am on the morning of George's 11th birthday. I couldn't go with David and I needed to be with George.

When I woke George on his birthday to say Happy Birthday and to tell him that David had been taken to hospital I was expecting tears, but George can be very surprising like that. He just accepted it for what it was and we carried on with the day. We did the zoom call and the family call and everyone rallied round with big smiles on their faces. George went to bed saying that he had had the best day and he sent David a message telling him that he loved him. My heart, which I thought couldn't break into any smaller pieces, broke all over again. It meant the world to me that my husband and my son were in accord.

I had become a master at hiding my feelings, my brave face was sometimes so brittle that the smallest thing could shatter it, and yet, on other occasions, it was the strongest support in the world – something to hide behind. Throughout the course of the day, I had been talking to the medical team in North Devon District Hospital and David was undergoing scans which had determined that he had got a twisted colon and would need urgent surgery. After I had put George into bed, I called the team and David was due to for surgery imminently. I sat, curled up on the settee, a glass of wine in my hand and had the most frank and honest discussion with the most wonderful surgeon. I explained that David was on about month five of GBM and the chemo was starting to take its toll, the red form (do not resuscitate) was signed and I was trusting her to do what was best for David and for our family. I told her I knew what death from glioblastoma could look like and I knew I had to get my son through it. If it was touch and go on the table, I asked her to make a call and that call should be to let him go. It was better for him to die well and at peace than to die a horrible and drawn-out death witnessed by his son. The surgeon was wonderful and accepted what I was saying graciously. After the call I felt strangely at peace as I had done the best I could for David and I knew he was in safe hands. It was almost the same feeling I had when I prayed at the alter in our church all those years ago. I lit candles and phoned Penny, our great friend and vicar; and we talked. I can still remember it so clearly, the calm words of love and support coming down the phone line to me. The candlelight softly lighting the room. The feeling of peace. I sat down to wait in the silence and stillness – all apart from the candles and the log fire crackling in the background.

Amazingly it wasn't long before I got a call from the team. David's operation had been a remarkable success and he was fine. I have never heard such relief in a person's voice than that surgeon. She hadn't had to make the call; she'd kept someone's husband and father alive. A few days later, David came home and we resumed normal life.

The world was starting to open up again after COVID, There were still a lot more restrictions, but ever so slowly you could feel the world starting to move again. We could meet friends in small groups and we could range further from home. One of David's most happy times was going milking on Andrew and Rachel's farm. The repetitive action of attaching the milking sets was wonderful to David. He didn't have to talk a lot, he could watch, smile, and work peacefully alongside Andrew and the family. George would be off round the fields with Andrew and Rachel's children and I would have a catch up with Rachel. For our family it was such a peaceful time, a time of great faith, a time of being wrapped in love with no expectations. We also met friends up near The Froude Stone on Exmoor, we took our deck chairs and sat round in a (socially distanced!) circle and listened to the cuckoo and innumerable sky larks singing overhead – trying to locate the tiny speck in the dazzling blue of the sky. We met Louisa, Tash and families on the sand dunes at Braunton Burrows and went down them on sledges (which David loved) and it started to snow. Sand sledging in the snow – what more could you ask for? This is what David had asked for: making memories with friends and family.

.

Chapter Eighteen
'I'M TIRED'

But both David and I knew that things had changed. His recent operation had taken that little more out of him and he had slowed even more. His frustration levels were increasing and he was getting angry. I couldn't blame him, he was so very tired, his battle had been fought for a long time. Our joy was there but it was a small flame that flickered so easily at the merest breeze. My heart was heavy for him, looking into those trapped eyes, knowing that he was going to bed in pain but understanding he was going to go through the same thing again tomorrow – it was grinding him down, literally taking away his life force that was once so strong, so vibrant, so bright. He didn't always make rational decisions and he wasn't very safe around the house. He started on anxiolytics to try and calm him down and make him less anxious as his anxiety and short temper was irrational. But we were coping. He saw his friends and he went for walks. We took a day at a time.

David got through his February and March cycles of chemotherapy, finishing cycle eight on 7th March. He used to take it in the evening before bed and I remember him sat on the edge of the bed, tablets in his left hand, the tablets that I couldn't touch because of the toxicity, glass of water in his right hand. He just looked down at the tablets and said quietly that he was tired and that he had had enough. I walked round to his side of the bed, sat down next to him, put my arm around him, he leaned into me and I just held him, telling him that it was fine, I supported his decision and that I was there for him. There were tears, our shoulders were sagging through the burden of disease, the weight of decision and depth of sorrow. I kept repeating that I couldn't love him more. I must have said that a thousand times over the course of the next three months.

But there was also beauty in the acceptance that you will let nature take her course. The fight was over, the pretence that everything is going to be ok was gone – we could be completely honest with each other. The peace that comes with decision, the serenity that allows recognition that every moment is precious. We talked openly of David's death with each other. David wasn't afraid of dying, just how he was going to get there, and I promised that I would make it ok for him – that I would fight for all the right decisions – and he knew me well enough to know I spoke the truth.

We told George that Dad was stopping chemotherapy and we just needed to chill out as a family. We planned a summer of events, spending time in Northern Ireland, a trip to Center Parcs and we booked a mobile home to take us to the Bear Grylls Gone Wild Festival. I even got in touch with Bear's team and David got a phone message with Bear telling him to keep fighting and he would see him in August. It was a wonderful message to receive, and David was ecstatic! We started to arrange David's 40th Birthday party for the first weekend in July. It was something for us to aim for and it was getting towards the end of March, we thought we would make it – the local pub was arranged and family were booking flights for the first week in July. But fate seemed to have other ideas.

Chapter Nineteen
HOW WE KNEW

Everything changed at the start of April.

We had a dog, Trampus, who was the most wired springer spaniel ever known in the history of humanity. This dog could run at the speed of light and in the blink of an eye, he was away. We had done training; he had all the paraphernalia needed for a dog that just loved birds (sky larks were a particular favourite). David used to walk him but understood that he always had to have him on the lead in a certain place and have the tracker on him. I told him that time and time again and usually was able to check before he left the house. But one day David got out on a walk before I was able to check that everything was ok – I can still remember watching him go, from my office window, and not being able to call out as I was chairing a meeting. He came back with no Trampus. I asked him if he'd put him on the lead where he usually legged it and if he had put Trampus's tracker on. He'd forgotten both. For David, that was unusual – he would normally forget one, or his phone, or the ball…so something – but usually he knew when to get him on the lead. Trampus was gone for hours and David was beside himself. We were worried he would get hung up on the harness. In the evening Dad came to pick up George so we could go out again to look for him and as they were going home they tracked up a lane, and there was Trampus, sat in the gateway, fairly unrepentant.

David was also starting to get blurred vision on occasion and he'd stumbled a few times. Nothing significant or that caused any damaged to himself, but it was just different. Our carpets were taking a pounding as he couldn't hold a cup of tea straight, that type of thing. He was waking up with backache and a sore bottom. His left pupil was different than his right. Lots of little one-offs that in isolation meant nothing and could be written off, but together seemed to indicate something more sinister. Listening to changes, understanding when clinical symptoms presented themselves was something that I had become particularly adept at. David wasn't right – his behaviour had changed, I needed to get him checked.

Trying to get people to understand that losing a dog coupled with the occasional stumble and blurred vision meant that David was ill was quite difficult in the time of a pandemic. However, the urgency in my voice got through and I was told to head to North Devon Hospital where the cancer team would be waiting for him. When we got there it was a close call as to whether I would be allowed in with him due to COVID restrictions, but wild horses wouldn't have kept me away. Over the years I had learned to fight for what my gut felt right. It exhausted me – this constant alert of knowing that I had to say the right thing to make sure I could stay with him. I always asked David to keep quiet and let me do the talking. It seemed harsh but I knew that David would say that he was ok and not remember the details and so would be sent home again. I'm not criticising our health service, on the contrary, but it would have been like asking a child of six to talk to you about everything that had happened over the last two weeks, in detail. It was asking for the impossible. COVID was another minefield as usually no-one could go in with the patient, but luckily I was able to make them understand that he was not able to explain things for himself. On this occasion, David and I sat happily in a side room for a few hours joking and then he headed off for a CT scan. A few hours later the oncology nurse confidently told us that there was nothing on the scan and we could go home.

At this point I learned something else about myself. I didn't get annoyed when the medical team is doing the best they could. I could have told them that they were wasting their time with a CT scan, that David needed an MRI. I was not in the least bit surprised that we were sent home. But I knew that something was wrong. No-one could tell me that David was OK, I was 100% sure that there were changes.

I started to write down everything that was going on in greater detail in my diary and was sending a daily update to our medical team. And things began to go downhill drastically. David was unable to read, he was losing focus, his vision was blurred, headaches awful, his back, neck and bottom were numb and his bottom and lower back were in considerable pain in the morning, his speech was slurred, he was fitting in his sleep and he was cold. He continually worried about going to the toilet, he was anxious, and he was constantly tired. I spoke to the oncologist one morning and we were discussing leptomeningeal disease (LMD) which is a cancer that is hideously difficult to pick up as it is in your cerebrospinal fluid and leptomeninges, the membranes around your brain and spinal cord. The time of diagnosis to death is usually four to six weeks. What we suspected was happening. This was everything that I had longed for and dreaded for over a decade. This was the end of David's life.

.

Chapter Twenty
THE LAST TRIP HOME

David was ok, he was quiet, but he was ok. It was best to let him find his way through this. His world shrank to our perimeter of our house and garden. He liked to get out, but he was worried about getting back so we went together, we went for a walk around the churchyard, he picked out a place he would like to be buried, he asked me if I would plant daffodils on his grave. We held hands, we had precious moments together.

David wanted to go home to Northern Ireland one last time which seemed to me like an herculean effort, but what David wanted, he got. So we obtained approval to travel during lockdown and purchased tickets for mid-May, George was allowed the time off school, I arranged special assistance at the airport and we were ready to go. But David continued to go downhill and the medical team were worried about David making the journey and asked if we could pull it forward a couple of days. It was stark to know we were talking in days. But David didn't understand the urgency and so we kept the dates the same. In a selfish way, I wanted to have the experience of being with David and George in Northern Ireland one last time. Seeing his face light up when he saw family, knowing that he was back where he belonged.

When we got to the airport David insisted on walking through security, he was never one for any fuss and could get quite belligerent if a matter was pushed. However, when we got through security he started to drag his legs and slur his words. We had George with us, the pressure I was under was immense and I was starting to panic, what if David fell? He wouldn't be allowed to fly. George was just at that age when he couldn't cope with things being different. I made David sit down and went to find security who scooped David up in a wheelchair and took him to a safe area. David was wearing his bag and he was struggling to manage it by himself so we would cram ourselves into the toilet and drain it together which is really difficult when you have nothing to drain it into and David had problems standing, let alone balancing on one leg which he needed to do so we could drain it into a toilet (it's just occurred to me that we could have unstrapped it from his leg…but that's the type of thing that you don't think about at the time). This constant battle of David adapting to his illness and disabilities, in combination with him understanding his limitations was one of the hardest things I had to watch.

Cognition was difficult for David and simple things like understanding when to turn his phone and iPad to aeroplane mode didn't sink in. He didn't understand why he had to do it and he was getting distressed that he couldn't get a connection but wouldn't let me touch his iPad, so I just left it – and he fell asleep as the plane took off. Naturally, David being David decided he needed to go to the toilet (forgetting his bag) just before the lights went on for the seat belts on descending. He got to the toilet but didn't emerge so one of the stewards let me go and see if he was ok, drawing the curtain round the toilet for privacy. When we opened the door, David was slumped over the sink trying to get his trousers up. Putting a brave face on whilst wanting to cry with upset for him was becoming a daily occurrence. He tried so hard to be normal, to maintain grace in the face of unimaginable horrors. I think the toilet did upset him though as he let us take him off the plane in a wheelchair and we went out to meet David's sister to take us home.

When we arrived, George went out with his uncle, Leslie on the farm, David slept like a baby and I inhaled a bottle of wine with

David's most wonderful sister Karen – having handed the baton of care to them. Accepting help is both a challenge and a blessing; David was so fiercely independent but independent in the way that he would let me do things for him but no one else was to know or to offer to help themselves. It was draining for me, but Karen and Leslie understood and I was able to relax and take some time to recharge my empty batteries.

Our days in Northern Ireland were lovely, they were filled with love, light and laughter. David, Karen, and I walked down to see the cows and then just about managed to get David home – it was only across two fields but we were a little worried we'd bitten off more than we could chew! But David made it. We had the family over and took lots of photos. David just sat there smiling, beaming in fact, he absolutely adored his family. He just watched everything carry on around him, letting the conversation wash over him and around him. Goodbyes weren't difficult as the family were coming over in a few weeks for David's birthday. If anyone thought that David wasn't going to make it, they didn't say. On the way home David gave in gracefully and we had a wheelchair from the moment that we arrived at the airport to home. We were looked after so well by the special assistant teams at both Bristol and Belfast International airports. It really is the little things in life really make a difference: the person that doesn't mind waiting that extra few minutes to allow David plenty of time to get his bearings; the smiles and friendly conversation when we were reeling about David being unable to walk; the careful positioning of David's wheelchair so that he couldn't see people staring at him; not minding when George was unable to speak because his brain couldn't compute the strangeness of seeing his Dad being wheeled around and not being able to talk, but looking at me with large, scared, uncomprehending eyes; the person that gave me a minute when I couldn't help the tears coming into my eyes and had lost the ability to carry on a conversation without a hitch in my voice. The compassion of those people knew no measure and I will be forever grateful to them.

Chapter Twenty - One
THE TRANSITION

When we got home the wheels of help ramped up a gear. It was the 17th May and I didn't realise that David would have less than two weeks to live. I arranged for walking aids, for care to help him get up, he had a garden kneeler as a temporary shower stool. We arranged for a hospital bed to be delivered to Blakesville. I got a list of help numbers as long as my arm. The day after we got back from Northern Ireland I knew we were fairly close to the end, but I didn't know how long we had got, so I called Karen and asked her to come as she needed to be with David as much as either George or I did. My sole focus was on keeping George emotionally stable and supported and keeping David as relaxed and pain-free. One of the conversations that is indelibly imprinted on my brain is a discussion with David's oncologist where I remember telling him that I needed to get David off this planet as quickly and as pain-free as possible: because I had two clear priorities: giving David a good death and minimising any damage to George as he would be watching his father die.

Karen arrived on the 18th May. My father had gone to Bristol to pick her up and she rolled in the front door as "Dad-Cabs" had taken a bottle of white wine and, as a nervous flier, Karen had inhaled the bottle on landing and during the ninety-minute drive home! Karen is the most unflappable person I know. She arrived at Blakesville in her steady (well, slightly unsteady on this occasion after a bottle of wine!) and undaunted way, without a moment of fuss or unnecessary drama. We also had another partner in crime, my cousin Tracey. So, the three of us tackled everything at home – Karen and Tracey taking it in turns to look after David, keep George amused and help me with the life admin that needed to go on. The days were warm and sunny, they passed by at the speed of light. In amongst the endless doctor's calls, nurse visits, medication deliveries, were flowers, cards, hampers, hugs. Messages of love and support. All were needed, all were welcomed, all were appreciated.

During David's last few days of being with us mentally, we had some very special moments even though his cognition was declining swiftly. We had decided that David was going to come off his steroids and he didn't want me to help him get them out of his pill box…so he got them all out and put them on the bedside table, I left him to it. Walking passed a short while later I saw them all in a pile by the bed and didn't think anything of it. Penny and her husband, John, were coming for communion and I called to David to let him know they had arrived. He came downstairs unaided and proceeded to take part in the service, reading the words, taking communion. I genuinely thought it was a miracle, that God had given David strength. However, when I went upstairs later in the day, the whole pile of steroids was gone, David had taken a week's worth in one sitting, no wonder he was on top form! But that, to me, is how God works: giving us the tools to have strength when we need it. It was funny, poignant, and loving, all at the same time.

When the hospital bed arrived, we put it on our landing, overlooking the valley where David could feel the sun on his face and a fresh breeze. I had received hospital bedding which was slippery to help manoeuvre David around the bed, but I wanted to keep crisp, cotton linen on the bed as wanted to keep things normal for him, what was good for him in life would be good for him in death. So, his new 'bedroom' was made up with bunches of flowers on the windowsill, cards, and messages of faith to keep him strong.

There was nothing that David couldn't have. Sunday, the 23rd May was our last night in bed together and I held him tight, we had decided he would be moving to the hospital bed the next day. He was unable to move around with ease but he was determined to try. Karen and I fitted a stair gate to the top of the stairs to stop him walking down unaided. Little did we know that he would never have the strength to walk down them again.

Life is made up of small moments: first times, last times, best times, worst times. These last few days were full of these: the last conversation we had together, the last television programme we watched, the last words he spoke, the last medication he took. These tend to be innocuous, everyday things which suddenly become implanted in your brain: changing the way you view things forevermore. Leaving memories that, in years to come, will transport you back in a matter of moments, to those times when your soul is ripped open, raw, for the whole world to see... unknowing that those same memories will cause the same reaction years in, years out. I have a woollen scarf that I wrapped around his hips to help keep his dignity after a catheter was fitted but we couldn't get clothes on him. *SAS: So You Think You Are Tough Enough* (David loved it!) was the last programme we watched together and I don't think I will ever be able to bring myself to watch it again. I know the friends that he told me he wanted to see before he couldn't remember who they were any more.

Once David moved into his new bed the care package we arranged started and teams came in once or twice a day. We had our hospice nurse and the district team on standby. David, it didn't matter who it was, would greet everyone with a beaming smile and a laugh...he was a natural born flirt with the charm of the (Northern!) Irish. Even when he didn't really understand what was being said or what was happening, his lovely face would light up with happiness and his rosy cheeks would blossom. Even as he slowly released his tenuous grip on life, his smiled dimmed but was still there. And whilst David smiled, I found I didn't need to cry.

Chapter Twenty-Two
THE FINAL DAYS

And David knew when to pull it out of the bag. In the last week of David's life George got very upset because his Dad didn't know his name anymore. But David didn't know anyone's name. However, the last person he called by name was his son, the last person he spoke to was George. George came back home from school early one day as he needed to be at home and Karen and I couldn't get David to swallow his oramorph, so George asked if he could give it a go…and David swallowed. I can remember saying under my breath 'well done DC'. He managed, even when he was only partly conscious, to make sure things were right for George. David's love for George knew no boundaries: it was pure, unfailing, and given freely and unreservedly. I know that David is watching George from heaven and is proud of the man that he is becoming.

In the last couple of days David had a syringe driver fitted and before he did, I invited a couple of our best friends to see him. These were amazingly hectic times with people coming and going, the phone never stopped. But around David's bed was peaceful and filled with light and love. As David's inner light faded, the house paused, waiting.

David's last day on this earth was another beautiful day. George had decided not to go to school; we were all very aware that we were near the end. All his medication had been withdrawn and he was only on pain relief and anti-epileptic meds through the syringe driver. The hospice team had arrived and were giving him a wash. But I had missed one thing: the anti-seizure meds in the driver were not strong enough. David went into a prolonged fit which I heard and recognised from the kitchen. Running upstairs I explained what was happening to the team and we called an ambulance and got him safe, with us all standing round the bed so he couldn't fall off. We waited for the ambulance. And bless them, we got two teams to help us. I had administered some rescue medication and he slowly came round. But he was in pain and one arm in particular seemed to be bothering him. His breathing was quite ragged and he was obviously not comfortable. I don't believe he ever recovered from his prolonged seizing. In the evening, when all was quiet again I sat on the side of the bed and told him that it was ok, he needed to give it up and leave us, we would be ok.

Later that evening David was still very uncomfortable and the medical team arrived to run through next steps. We decided to increase his morphine to try and get his pain under control. David was completely unresponsive to us but he was obviously still able to feel pain. When the morphine increased David was more peaceful. And again, the house settled down for the night. We had a nurse to sit with David overnight so that Karen and I could get rest and Leslie, Karen's husband arrived via "Dad-Cabs" at midnight. All the people that David needed around him and wanted to be with him were there. He was at peace. I kept repeating that I couldn't love him more, I stroked his face and I told him that he could leave us, that he could go. And then we went to bed.

I woke again a couple of hours later with a feeling and I went out onto the landing to check on David. His breathing was shallow and I knew we were there, so I woke Karen and we just spent some time with him. I then went to wake George and told him it was time to say goodbye. I was stood at his head and George and Karen were to one side. I placed my hands on David's head and said The Lord's Prayer in my head. And as I said it, I felt David's soul leave his body.

There was no more pain.

.

Chapter Twenty-Three
IN PREPARATION FOR THE LAST GOODBYE

My experiences of a death in Northern Ireland were completely opposite to that of one in England and I was always a little worried about how I was going to navigate the cultural complexities. But Karen and Leslie, again were amazing and just let us find our way. There was a backlog of funerals post COVID and David's funeral was planned for the 12th June. In a way this was good as it gave us time to prepare. I wanted to make David's funeral the 40th party that he had not had, a time to celebrate his life, but a proper time to say goodbye. I wanted to make it unique to David and the wonderful man he was, but also comfortable for George. I wanted it to be a Christian service, but not too sombre. We were allowed to have a church service as long as we kept within the safe distancing guidelines that the church allowed. Ironically, David had been one of the people that had helped decide what the safe numbers were.

But firstly, I needed to thank people and fill my days, so my trusty wonderful sisters-that-are-not-sisters, Karen and Tracey and I took ourselves off into the local town to fill hampers for the hospice and nursing teams. Never once did they say: are you mad? Do you need to be doing this right now? They just accepted and loved me, and just let me do my thing. David would have wanted it.

David and I had decided on coffins many years ago and I kept true to that. George chose what David would wear so he had his Northern Ireland rugby top, tracksuit bottoms that he was comfortable in, his Spurs scarf and his football boots that he used to wear to play with George. He was buried with his bee outfit, his mother's cross, a piece of felt that I had made, which he loved, as his pillow. He loved his Lego figures…they went in with him. He had everything he loved and was special to him. In the top of the coffin, I didn't want flowers, so our wonderful friend, Anne, who had done our wedding cake and George's Christening cake (and a myriad of birthday cakes!) did us a 'coffin topper'. This coffin topper was of David, holding a cross, with one of the spaniels sat with him with some sheep and deer. I had got a stone from the area round the Froude Stone where David loved to walk. We surrounded the coffin topper with beautiful flowers – it looked stunning and so very 'David', he would have loved it. We put the last couple of mini-Lego figures: a rabbit and a deer on top. One last thing that Anne simply didn't have time to make were a couple of cows (hardly surprising!), so Karen, Leslie, Colin, and I made them out of gingerbread and popped a couple round to Andrew and Rachel, our church and milking friends…as ginger is Andrew's favourite.

Organising the seating in the church was humbling, delightful and tragic all at the same time. We had so many messages of love and support from across the world. We had flowers on every windowsill in the house and we even filled his wellies with water and put bouquets in them and stood them in the porch. And the number of people that wanted to come were the same as the messages – too numerous to count. In the Post-COVID world we needed to name pews, count numbers, name names, so we organised around family groups, we sat the more elderly church goers in the choir stalls, the furthest from the congregation. And because we could be that specific, I was able to print photos of David with people that were going to be in the pews: at adventure parks, rugby, surfing a sand dune, making silly faces, dressed as an angel in a nativity play, hugging, laughing, just loving life. And for those that I couldn't find a personal photo, I chose my favourite; David holding a cross, a photo taken from his 'better' side- you couldn't see the evidence of the tumour, he was holding a cross and he was smiling: peace flowed out of his gentle eyes. I still have the photo up today and when I go to see my friends, I quite often see a copy lodged on a windowsill or a sideboard.

One of the traditions in Northern Ireland is to visit the funeral home, but I couldn't bring myself to do that. I had told David I loved him before he left Blakesville. I had stroked his cancer-beaten, pain-worn face that was at peace and told him I would always love him and that I would look after our son. I couldn't see him cold and lifeless. I let George decide if he wanted to see him and he chose not to. I am glad he did. But my Mum took Karen and I asked them to check if he was ok. He was.

David, our vicar had seen us through the worst of times and he came off sabbatical to welcome David into church for the last time. Penny was leading the funeral service but both were there to see David come to church on the evening of 11th June. Karen and I met David, Penny, and David at the lychgate and we processed into church where a simple service was held and it gave Karen and I the chance to say our goodbyes in peace. It was an extremely sacred time for me and the solace I got from receiving the strength from David, Penny and Karen will never be underestimated. Then, we lit candles and Christian music, just as David would have wanted, played peacefully as David lay at the altar, ready for us to say our goodbyes. And in the evening, when the family arrived, they got the chance to come and see David, resting peacefully, and to say their prayers with him. It was a time of brain numbing grief but also a time of love and the tiny awakening of healing.

.

Chapter Twenty-Four
'THERE WILL BE NO TEARS'

David's funeral was beautiful June day; the birds sung, the sun shone, and all was good with the world. I was up early and went to check that David had a restful night. The church was peaceful and at rest. David had spent his last night in one of the places that he loved the most.

David's order of service was another thing that a considerable amount of thought had gone into. Its cover and back was as plain as I could make it, but when you opened the order of service, it was filled with light, laughter, smiles and (to be honest) David being daft....and just David. I loved it and I still do. The flowers in the church were simple and just around the Paschal Candle – the same candle that David had accidentally left lit one night and then went back the next day and it was burned down. The photos looked welcoming, the church had her arms open and the ancient stones were warmed with the summer sun. Everything was just right.

One of my main concerns was George. I needed to get him through the day with the minimum of upset. He had laid out his carefully chosen clothes in our room (or my room? what do you say after someone has died?) with a note saying 'Funeral Clothes' - I still have the note. He was the bravest boy I knew and I was so proud of him. Even the day of David's death he went to school. School had been brilliant, watching and caring for him so carefully. But I could see that his grief was just under the surface. But he coped, and I will always admire him for his resilience. We had arranged the funeral to be considerate of him as far as we could. We didn't have a procession into church (after all David was there) and at the end of the service everyone would leave and then we would go for a private burial. It worked perfectly. We were in a front pew so no-one (bar the choir stalls) could see him. It was just me and him in the pew and he only needed to look round when he wanted.

Penny led the service beautifully, but I couldn't tell you what she said. I was in the adrenaline bubble. I read the eulogy I'd been preparing in my head for the last decade and got through it. The music I chose was not what David and I had discussed, but what was right for the time – Bethel Music's '*The Blessing*', Stuart Townend's version of '*The Lord's My Shepherd*' and amazing song by Ghost Ship '*The Revelation of Jesus Christ*. It spoke perfectly for, and of, David.

After the service everyone filtered out. I was later told that a single buzzard was circling the church tower in the thermals rising from the ground. Make of that what you will but it brought be comfort and it meant a lot to be told. We buried David in the spot that David and I had discussed, and Karen and I have since planted daffodils. There was a small gathering: just Penny, Karen and Leslie, David's two best friends, Malcom and Andrew, Louisa and Rachel, and Elsie. I stood there, with one arm round Elsie, the other round George, watching as Malcolm and Andrew lowered David into his grave and all I could think was: how on earth are they doing that without burning their hands with the ropes! A fairly irreverent thought but perhaps that's what keeps you sane!

David's grave was left like his life. He had a wonderful giant windmill that Tracey had bought and we all had one for our gardens to watch and think of him, a wooden cross and flowers. Beautiful, bright and happy.

David was at peace.

.

Chapter Twenty-Five
AFTERWARDS

On the 16th June, Karen and Leslie returned to Northern Ireland and I prepared to face life. On the 17th June, we had our old dog, Brandy, put to sleep. Brandy was the puppy that David and I got before we moved to Devon and he had seen me through the worst times. The occasions were too numerous to count when I had sat with Brandy, clinging to him, and he patiently sat as my tears soaked into his coat. But I could do for Brandy what I couldn't do for David. He was suffering and I had the power to relieve him of that in a way that I couldn't for David. And weirdly, having Brandy gone seemed to even up the balance with David and Brandy in heaven, and George, Trampus, and I on earth. It still surprises me how much peace that thought brings me.

We started to enter the dark, dark days of overwhelming waves of grief. George was going to school, I was working, and I stumbled through the days, not really having a clue what was happening. I didn't seem to be able to get George in the right school uniform (which is never cool). I would be scrabbling around trying to find trousers or a polo shirt that was not wet nor in the washing machine. Always a competent cook, I didn't seem to be able to get food on the table. I could never get the bins out on the right day. And there didn't seem to be a reason why I couldn't as nothing had changed;

school was school, food was in the cupboard, bin day was still bin day, but I didn't seem to be able to join the dots.

But I felt I did quite well in the crying department (in my opinion!) until Sunday morning of the first weekend. I had been warned that weekends are the worst and I thought I would cope. But about 11am I collapsed. I just couldn't bare him not being here. He *should* be here. He should be here with *me*. I remember calling my parents and collapsing in a heap. It was almost like they were waiting for the call. They were right round and we did gardening, housework, chatted, cried, and swore…everything that I needed to do. And then they left so that I could learn to start being alone with George. George was dry eyed, shell shocked, not sure of anything; but needing continuity and surety. I tried my best to give him that.

And all our friends were amazing and so were acquaintances. Louisa and Tash, who know me so well, my most intimate friends, knew that I needed to find myself again. They were there at a text, a call; ready to make a plan. They still are. But then there were others, like Mezzi, like Celia, like Sherry, that messaged and sensed the tone of the reply, or even lack of response, and in the next moment were knocking on my door or stopping me in the village square, to talk to me about loss and how they were there for me.

And George, it's difficult to say. He appeared to cope so well on the outside, so resilient, so strong. But he needed me to be close. Not as close as in the past, but close. And I wanted to be there. School and family were his mainstays, his rock to cling to. There is no easy way to navigate grief with a child, but I took my measure from him. I have come to the conclusion that there is no wrong nor right way of helping a child cope with grief, no roadmap to follow. I wish there was. There are books to read, advice to listen to, processes to follow, but none fit exactly right. No two situations the same. And you don't get a test run at this, rarely do people get the chance to hone their skills a second time and how awful would that be? So, we stumbled along together, groping through the darkness, straining to find a light at the end of our tunnel. There is so much to say about George, but my thoughts are so jumbled in my mind and if I can't even sort them out in my own head and get them on paper, as an adult, how is he meant to understand himself? But we took every day as it came, me trying to objectively assess how he was doing whilst navigating my own grief; a time when objectivity and dissociation seems to be unattainable. I put aside my own feelings, my desire to curl up in a ball and stay very still and I put on the brave face, the mask that was there for the world to see. But the tears wouldn't stop. Once George had a couple of friends over for the day and I was sat reading, tears pouring down my face – those huge ones that seem to be the size of a small ocean. The three of them came and asked if they could have a sleep over. I remember just saying: Yes, as long as you don't mind me crying. It sounds dreadfully miserable as I write, but it wasn't at the time as it was said with a smile. And one by one they just filed over and gave me a hug: unprompted but so very welcome.

Those first few weeks I stumbled through, and somewhere, somehow, I saw this:

As for grief, you'll find it comes in waves. When the ship is first wrecked, you're drowning, with wreckage all around you. Everything floating around you reminds you of the beauty and the magnificence of the ship that was, and is no more. And all you can do is float. You find some piece of the wreckage and you hang on for a while. Maybe it's some physical thing. Maybe it's a happy memory or a photograph. Maybe it's a person who is also floating. For a while, all you can do is float. Stay alive.

In the beginning, the waves are 100 feet tall and crash over you without mercy. They come 10 seconds apart and don't even give you time to catch your breath. All you can do is hang on and float. After a while, maybe weeks, maybe months, you'll find the waves are still 100 feet tall, but they come further apart. When they come, they still crash all over you and wipe you out. But in between, you can breathe, you can function. You never know what's going to trigger the grief. It might be a song, a picture, a street intersection, the smell of a cup of coffee. It can be just about anything…and the wave comes crashing. But in between waves, there is life.

Somewhere down the line, and it's different for everybody, you find that the waves are only 80 feet tall. Or 50 feet tall. And while they still come, they come further apart. You can see them coming. An anniversary, a birthday, or Christmas, or landing at O'Hare. You can see it coming, for the most part, and prepare yourself. And when it washes over you, you know that somehow you will, again, come out the other side. Soaking wet, sputtering, still hanging on to some tiny piece of the wreckage, but you'll come out.

Take it from an old guy. The waves never stop coming, and somehow you don't really want them to. But you learn that you'll survive them. And other waves will come. And you'll survive them too. If you're lucky, you'll have lots of scars from lots of loves. And lots of shipwrecks.[2]

And it summed up perfectly how I felt and how I still feel.

David's grave became a lifeline to me, and I visited it religiously. The windmill was still on the grave and as the wind blew it spun frantically, and David would have loved it. It became significant to me, as I walked around the corner of the church, if I saw it spinning in the wind I knew he was there. Many years ago, when George was a toddler, I had come out of church (because he was too active to sit through an entire Sunday service) and in the churchyard was a young woman. She had spread out a blanket by a grave and was reading a book and drinking from a thermos cup. She remains in my mind, to this day, and I wanted that peace when I saw David's grave. So, Pip, Tash's wonderful partner, put a log stump at the end of the grave for me to sit. Day in day out I visited, looking for the spinning windmill to know that he was there. And inevitably it was with the green blades whirling around in the breeze.

Some days I couldn't contain my grief and the need to be close to David. One morning I remember going up to see David before 7am and I wandered up in my dressing gown (it was a lovely, soft knit – don't worry!) and my pjs (which were a very skimpy bra and shorts set – not so flattering!). I laid on his grave, my head at his head and my toes at his toes. I felt the earth connect us through the

[2] *u/GSnow, circa 2010, Grief Comes in Waves,*
https://www.reddit.com/r/Assistance/comments/hax0t/comment/c1u0rx2/

cool, soft grass on my back, and I rested. I don't know how long I lay there, but the next thing I knew there was sniffs around me and some frantic dog calling under someone's breath. It was one of the villagers come to walk the graveyard early. He must have thought I was totally mad, but I didn't mind. I stood up, apologised for my attire and we had a lovely chat. Shortly after that his dog cocked his leg on David's cross, much to the owner's embarrassment and amusement from me. David loved dogs; he wouldn't mind that. He would have embraced the moment just as it was – raw, unadulterated nature.

But David hadn't quite left us. I saw small flashes of light in the utility and the hall. They were always just outside the room and it was almost as if a small shaft of light moved. It was a fraction of a second and the best way I can describe it is as if mirrored door was closed and the movement of reflected light across the room catches your eye. It happened in places that no light shaft could reach. One evening I was sitting at the kitchen having a cup of tea with Mezzi and I saw it. I just put my head in my hands and told her I thought I was going mad and explained to her why. And Mezzi just said, very gently, 'You're not going mad, I have seen it too'. It wasn't scary and I saw it for a couple of months and then never again. But I choose to believe that it was the pre-tumour David, just taking care of us and checking we were ok. When he knew we were learning to live again, when he saw that I could smile with my eyes, he left us to be at peace.

.

Part IV

Learning to Adapt

Chapter Twenty-Six
SHACKLES OFF

There is no timeframe for grief. I feel that we were incredibly lucky with David's form of brain cancer as we lost him slowly over time, an insidious creep of destruction that allowed us to mourn gradually. Every milestone of decline was another period of grief, as a loss of David's life, George's life, and our lives together. I once heard someone mention in a work meeting that their tumour was attached to many more people than just themselves and that was so true. But the death of David's brain tumour gave me life again. I knew that David was watching over us, whole again.

And I adapted. I bought more school uniform so that I had more time to get things through the wash. I signed up to one of those pre-prepared food companies that deliver kits to your door. I tried to finish work at a reasonable time. I took George to his clubs and we saw more of my parents. Within a couple of months, I was like a different person and I am not going to lie - I felt rejuvenated and alive. For the first time in years, I could live my life. I didn't have to go out with bags of tablets and changes of clothes. We could go where we wanted, with what we wanted, with hardly any notice. I went swimming with seals with a wonderful friend whose husband had also died of cancer. I went to Tracey's and spent the weekend on dog walks, in the hot tub, having BBQs and generally just being at ease.

As we headed into summer holidays, the trips that we had planned for 'David's last summer' approached and I decided that George and I would do them together. So, I contacted Ian, the wonderful man who had Trampus when David went to Plymouth for his second craniotomy and he agreed to have Trampus again. Ian and I talked, and messaged, and talked and messaged, and over the summer Ian and I fell in love. Whilst Trampus stayed with Ian in Cornwall, George and I went Scotland, Northern Ireland, Center Parcs and the Bear Gryll's Gone Wild Festival. We met Bear who signed all David's Bear books, for George to keep (and Bear gave George the *best* hug). And in between trips, Ian and I would meet and by the time we were heading into Autumn, Ian became part of our family.

I bought new clothes, I smiled at the sun, I didn't drink wine (a first for me!), and I exercised again. I cleaned out David's clothes just keeping the ones that were special to us. I threw away tablets, urine bags, mattress protectors, pill boxes, piles of things that David had collected, old papers - all the things that David didn't let go. I remembered the pre-tumour David and not how he was after the tumour took hold.

George settled; he had a need to have familiar people around him, he wanted continuity and familiarity. He didn't want change. But he loved spending time with Nana, Grandpa, Karen, Leslie, Tracey, Louisa, Malcolm and Elsie, Rachel, Andrew (and the family), Ian and his pack of eight dogs – all the steady people (and animals!) in his life. Those that he could trust and he knew were 100% in his camp.

I learned to say that my husband had died from a brain tumour. The more confident I was and the more factual, the more people accepted it, were less awkward, and were able to talk themselves which I found better because I wanted to talk. I wanted to be open and I didn't want David assigned to memories. Talking about him kept him alive for me; it still does.

Chapter Twenty-Seven
TIME BRINGS PEACE

But that 'de-mob' happy feeling didn't last passed the first year. The second year I found being without David so much more difficult and more challenging. As my emotions settled, I found myself reliving his life and starting to have regrets and getting incredibly angry. I was starting to come to terms with the loss, and the emotions associated with grief and loss were catching up with the emotions associated with freedom and life.

I have cried those hot, bitter tears that have scalded my cheeks. I am angry of the injustice of such a wonderful, kind man being taken. It has been like losing a child. David was my child and my husband. He had such an innocent outlook on life. No-one should lose a child. I still reel from this and it is the one thing that makes me more cry more than anything else. I just wish he was here. He loved life. He was happy. He was innocent.

I regretted putting everyone first before my own needs in the last week of his death. I didn't have time to really sit with him and say goodbye. I regretted saying on his last day to increase his morphine. If I hadn't said that, would I have had longer with him? Would I have been able to hold his warm hand longer? Place my hand on his chest and feel him breathe?

I worried about falling in love again so soon. I worried about what the people in our community said about it. I worried about what David's family would think. I worried whether my love was just a rebound and that it wouldn't last.

I don't want to say that time is a good healer, but I do believe that time brings peace, acceptance, and insight. Over time I realised that all my regrets were worthless and that they centred around me, not selfishly, but what I would have wanted and what I would have changed. But I have grown to learn that God took David when we were ready. As I started to accept my emotions as they were, I started to understand and accept; appreciating that I needed to let go of what I couldn't change.

Yes, I could have spent more time with him during his death, but the most important thing was that David had the good death that he wanted. The good death that I had told the oncologist that George needed. I gave him that. I gave people the gift of time to say goodbye. I was there when David needed me, I was there to tell him to leave us, and I was there to tell him we loved him and always would.

I could have kept his morphine lower which might have given us an extra day, but that wasn't guaranteed. And what would the quality of that day be? David was in pain and distress. Was an extra day kind to David? George already had more hideous pictures in his mind than any child needed at that age, did he need more? I wouldn't have been sitting there with him quietly, he would have been dragging rasping breaths into his ravaged body; neither of us being at peace. I would have been up and down, trying everything I could to keep David comfortable. Karen would have been swabbing and cleaning his mouth, something that I couldn't bring myself to do.

And I have learned not to worry about people talking about me and judging how I have acted after David's death. I know that I have acted respectfully and with love for David every moment of our lives together and that his memory is treasured. I can't change other people's opinion of me, but their discussions behind closed doors can't hurt me. I have learned who my true friends are and they understand it is possible to cry with bone shattering grief whilst your soul flies on the wings of love.

And my love for Ian is a real, lasting, deep, and wonderful thing. It wasn't a reaction; it was a touching of souls and we have met at the right time in our lives. We are good together and good for each other. Time has made me realise that I can love again. I will always choose love; I will always choose light; I will always choose to float.

.

Chapter Twenty-Eight
CHANGES

I have been irreversibly changed; the reality of repeated trauma and thirteen years of caring is going to leave lasting scars. I think I was naive to think it wouldn't. I am still learning to understand myself and work out whether I can live with the changes or whether I concentrate on changing again. But what I do know is that I need to be patient as there will be more changes over time. I am light years away from the unhinged person after David's death when the wheels really came off... but I am still a work in progress. When I read what I have written I have to concentrate on suspending judgement and emotion. It is just as it is. There is no right or wrong.

For a confident person I have incredibly low self-worth, I place little value on myself. When David was alive, both he and George needed me every hour of every day. I measured my worth in need. David needed me for all his decisions, advice, thoughts, and every action he verified. He literally couldn't survive without me. George needed me as a child needs his mother, for warmth, nourishment, and love. With David gone and George grown, no-one needed me (Ian is possibly the most independent person I know – apart from when it comes to technology!) and so I went from being asked questions all the time to nothing. I was not needed and my measurement of worth was gone. I am slowly learning that to be wanted is equally important as being needed. Ian has to repeatedly tell me that he is with me because he wants me, not because he needs me. It is hard for me to accept. But he has been incredibly patient and loving whilst I tell him what coat to wear out, what socks to put on, what to eat, and asking him if he's remembered his wallet. I think when he pointed out that, at his age, he was more than capable of choosing his outer layer was a defining point in our relationship! He also pointed out, quite patiently, that George has known for many years that he needs to put his shoes on before leaving the house. What was initially quite traumatic for me is something that I can now be gently teased about… and I am learning to laugh at the small things again.

I have been left with the need to have everything perfect all the time and the need to be stocked up in case of emergency. This year, again I have completed my Christmas shopping by mid-October. My fear of dropping a ball is real. I hold myself to levels of performance that I would expect no-one else to achieve. The understanding that I grant everyone else in my life I don't give myself. I don't watch television, I rarely sit down for an afternoon to read a book, and I don't leave work without all my emails read, actioned, and cleared from my inbox. When I get home from a business trip, I prepare the case to go again so all I need to do is add my clothes. I worry that the wheels will come off my life and therefore always need to be prepared.

Part of the brownie point/being prepared for everything left me with a difficulty in saying no. And I was saying yes to everyone – spreading myself so thin that I was always on the edge or tears and exhaustion. I still find saying no very challenging, but I am starting get better at it, with Ian's encouragement. I still help, but I keep myself out of situations that I know I will be called upon and that really helps. Penny gave me some wonderful advice; she told me to lock the door for a year after David died so that I had chance to find myself again. And I am slowly finding Clare again.

Weirdly, I won't go into a shop or a public place without an absolute need. If I do, I am in and out with no stopping. I will go without rather than have to leave the house for something. I avoid supermarkets. However, if someone else asks me to get something for them then I will do it without hesitation. I still have no idea why. I have no fear, I just don't want to be stopped and asked questions, I don't like the thought of being caught off guard. But if I do meet people I know then I love it. Ian does our supermarket drop-ins now – I can't even begin to work that out in my mind and, to be honest, it doesn't hurt anyone so I don't worry about it. I've learned that sometimes it's ok to be a bit weird!

But on the flip side of the coin, our house is stocked up to the gunnels with all sorts of necessities, in the case of emergencies: candles, long life milk, toilet roll, batteries, and tissues. I usually have four of everything, and if anything is less than half full a replacement is bought. I have food that will last about two months, I can make loaves for about a year, and toiletries that will see us into 2025. Our wonderful housekeeper, Sue, quite often shouts up to my office to tell me not to buy any more tomato-based products! The cars always have to be over half full of diesel (another thing that Ian is very patient with). I have enough washing powder and dishwasher tablets to last a year. I have a full pharmacy at home; guests have no fear that they will not receive treatment for diarrhoea, constipation, hangovers, headaches, burns, bites, bad backs or sprained knees. I have plasters that can cover a scratch or dressings that can patch up quite a severe gash. But I don't hoard; if I don't need something it is given away or recycled. I don't want anything that doesn't have a purpose.

But these are all harmless things and I learn to let them go. One day I may be more peaceful and realise that I don't have to have so much – that I can still be safe without it.

I am only now starting to realise now that my last thirteen years have been lived with a low level of anxiety that simply hasn't gone away. I find myself reacting to situations with a lot more volatility that is needed, especially if it is a trigger for a situation that has happened with David. These triggers occur at any time with absolutely no warning at all, but when they happen, my fear is real, my anxiety rockets and I feel my body flush with adrenaline. I am trying to unpick it piece by piece and learn to be gentle with myself, but it is not easy. I have found that my inner battery runs on empty more easily, I am more emotionally exposed, and more raw. I tire more easily, but in recognising that is a half the battle and I am learning to be kind to myself and accept myself for what I am.

I have learned that it isn't the birthdays and anniversaries that cause the unexpected tsunami of grief, but it is finding a Spurs facemask at the bottom of the drawer, it is smelling his aftershave that George now has (why do I do it I ask myself!?), it is seeing friends that knew David before his tumour, it is finding his old hospital pyjamas when I am clearing out the airing cupboard. When George kicked his first conversion for his new school I was so immensely proud to see it sail over the bar, but with that pride came soul-aching sadness and tears. Even though I know David is watching George, I just wanted him to be standing there beside me. To see his face light up.

But I know that David is there with George and I in spirit and I have learned to let the feelings wash over me, to appreciate them for the memories that they bring.

I have chosen to float.

Chapter Twenty-Nine
In Closing

I now have opportunity to travel the world and talk to people about David's death and how clinical research can benefit from the insights that we have from David's illness. As technology progresses, we no longer have to be in hospital to benefit from healthcare, and we can give people a better quality of life by letting them be at home whilst still maintaining the close relationships you need with a medical team. I love my job. I love finding solutions for our patients, because I can appreciate how fantastic medical support can change a person's life, and that of their support network. We have the potential to allow people a good death. The death that David had. The first time I talked in public was a virtual meeting to a conference in Philadelphia and after the meeting I was in pieces because I felt that David's death hadn't been in vain. And I know that David would want me to talk about his life. It keeps him alive for me – it gives me strength.

And through my journey I have my tribe with me: Ian, who leads me carefully and gently through my grief; George, who is perceptive to my every thought and feeling and who is growing into a man his father can be proud of; my parents, who love and are loved unreservedly; my sisters-who-are-not-sisters, Karen and Tracey, who I don't speak to that much but who are always there; and my friends,

Louisa and Tash, who accept and love me for who I am. I couldn't be without any of them and I thank them for everything they do.

Yes, I am on a different path than I thought my life would take. But now I can hold my head high, I have the confidence of age and of being a survivor, for that is what I am. I give and receive love unreservedly.

Our old vicar David once told us about Kintsugi, the Japanese art of mending broken pottery with gold, making a stronger and more beautiful pot than the original. I feel I have been repaired by Kintsugi. I have realised that it is ok to be happy again. I have faith in God and in myself, my fundamental ability to choose love, to choose faith, to choose light.

To float.

Appendix One

LIFE LESSONS

LIFE LESSONS

I thought I would write about some of the life lessons that I have learned through this time – unfortunately usually too late to benefit me at the time, but I hope this will be of some use in the future. I'm sure there are a lot of people that have a lot more knowledge on this, but fundamentally the principles boil down to the same thing; be kind to yourself and others, don't judge, and tell people you love them.

There is no right nor wrong

Everyone copes with grief and times of trauma in their own way. I kept myself very busy because I felt that if I dropped a ball then everything would come crashing down. I did my Christmas preparation in October, I have enough food in the house to survive the apocalypse, and my house was always perfect. I remember having a doctor to the house early one October and I had the Christmas puddings on the stove steaming – the whole house smelled of them. He looked at me as if I was mad. David was about to be ambulanced to hospital and I was cooking Christmas puddings. I had to explain that I made them and they had to be steamed before being re-wrapped and put away, I couldn't let them ruin – even if David was on death's door – as I wouldn't have time to do them again! After David died, I kept myself busy with the hamper preparation for the nursing staff. But that is my way of coping. It might not be anyone else's but I have learned to cope my own way. There is no right or wrong and don't listen to anyone who might judge.

Everyone is doing the best they can...honestly!

I remember going to one conference and thinking that I needed to remember how I crossed my legs when I was on stage. Why did I need to remember? Because I had only had time to shave one leg. So, I had to make sure my left leg was on top! It is madness to think back on it now... but people the world over are in the same place. Everyone is trying to get through the day in the best way they know how. Lots of people come across as in control, I know I do, but it can all be held together with a thread. Take the time to say people look good, that that colour suits them, that you are pleased to see them and looking forward to a catch up. It costs nothing to make someone feel good about themselves and give them a bit of a breather. Take the weight if and when you can. Be gentle, be kind.

Everything happens for a reason

When David and I left for London in March 2010, George stayed with my parents. Over the next five- or six-years Mum and Dad picked up and stepped in on every occasion that I needed help. But out of that has grown a bond of love between George and my parents that is so strong and unwavering. Grandpa is the first person that George runs to, and Nana is one of the only people allowed to hug him (high praise indeed as a teenager!) Those months of me worrying over how Trampus was being affected as a puppy led me to Ian. Whatever happens, good will always triumph over bad. It might be years down the line, but one day you will stop and say 'oh, so that's why that happened'. If you can believe that there will be a reason, sometimes it makes the more hideous times seem a little less scary. Trust, it is all about trust in the power of good. Have faith.

In times of stress, you are not yourself.

I'm not going to go into details, but two days before David died I got a fraudulent call from a person pretending to be my bank. I was on the phone to 'the bank' as well as taking another call. They managed to get three security codes out of me and took £27,000 out of my account before I told them that I couldn't talk any longer as David was literally dying and I would have to call them back. If you had asked me at the time, I would have told you I was in my perfectly sane mind with no issues at all – I know all about scammers and there was no chance that would happen to me. But it did. Because I was stressed. I learned that, in times of stress, no matter how much you feel you are on top of things, your judgement can be clouded. So, recognise that and be careful where you can. The banks and police were wonderful, as an aside, and the money was swiftly returned.

All feelings pass

We always remember when we are at the opposite ends of the emotional spectrum, but we always seem to remember the negative more than the positive. I remember hearing once that all emotions run in a cycle and we can either decide to jump on board with the emotion or let it go. So, if you feel anger, you join in with that emotion and boil over; if you feel despondent, if you engage, you get dragged down. You often hear people say things like, when I feel sad I go and do some gardening and it's the same: if you can distract yourself from the emotion, if you can choose not to engage, it will pass. I became adept at that and to this day I will happily stop Ian when the route he is taking with a conversation raises anxiety or upset; gently pointing out that this is not good for me. And I encourage everyone to do that. Recognise that it is in your power to engage or ignore a negative emotion and that you are in control. Whatever the emotion is, good, bad, or ugly; it will pass. Let it go.

It's not about brownie points

Over the period of David's illness, I spent a long time trying to accumulate brownie points: whether it be working fourteen-hour days, travelling for work at the weekend, giving lifts to friend's children, or having children overnight. As you can imagine, that's a lot of brownie points! In my head knowing that a time would come when I would need time off work or ask for help getting George to the right place at the right time and I never knew when I would need help. After David's death, I didn't use the brownie points. I went back to work before David's funeral and, within a couple of weeks after the funeral, offers of help dried up because people had their own lives to get on with and I was too proud to ask, scared of getting rebuffed. On one occasion a friend messaged, quite innocently, to tell me that George no longer had a place in her car and could I contact another parent to see if they could take George to a football match. I was left trying to juggle those balls that I couldn't drop and the message reduced me to tears of hopelessness and overwhelming perception that life was beating me and was never going to learn how to cope.

I don't think I would do the same again, I now understand that it is more important to spend time with the people that matter and put those that you love first. I ended up frazzled trying to be all things to all people and the people that needed me: David and George, actually only got half of me – and it was the tired, life-worn, over stretched person. So, I learned to keep healthy boundaries; treat others in the way that I wished to be treated and be true to myself. I learned that if I found myself going out of my way to do something that I didn't have time for or really didn't want to do, it probably wasn't going to do me any good.

Value your true friends

My parents said to me once that you can count your good friends on one hand, and with the benefit of hindsight I would possibly extend that to two hands. Good friends will be there for you thick and thin, and I also found that people that I knew as acquaintances would move heaven and earth to be there for me. Gentle friendships that showed understanding and allowed me to be me came to the fore were the balm to the friends that I thought would be there and weren't. If people don't act in the way that you thought they would, then let it go.

The strength that some of my friends showed, particularly close friends was amazing. They were hurting as much as me but they were there for me, and they always looked to me first. Penny: who not only was one of David's closest friends, who gave David his last communion, who stood and took his funeral service, was always there with a laugh and a hug. Malcolm and Andrew, who lowered David's coffin into the ground, were there helping me when I needed it. Louisa, who put her North Devon Hospice Mission Unbreakable medal on David's grave was there at the end of every message – ready to drink wine and be my biggest advocate. The list goes on. It is easy to lose sight of others grieving when you are in the midst of your own and I will never forget how much that meant to me.

Preserve your strength and sense of self

On many occasions I felt helpless and angry with the situation we were in and life just felt unjust. I genuinely believe when the world just feels like your feet are stuck in treacle and you can't move with the tiredness of life, you should stop, take a day or two to recover and then realise that there are only two ways to go: down or up. Unfailingly we went up, because for us, there was no choice. No choice but to carry on. I found a quote once by Bob Marley and it struck me: 'You never know how strong you are, until being strong is your only choice'. There was never a truer word. But I need time to be that Weeble, that 1970s egg-shaped toy, to be at the bottom before slowly bouncing back. The beauty is understanding that you need to learn to be kind to yourself, be gentle and understand that invisible wounds take time to heal as well.

Naturally, I am a person that wants to be by themselves. I don't like confrontation and I like to be on good terms with everyone. There were times when I was pushed down a blind alley until I had no choice but to turn and fight. The time when I was most vitriolic was in Plymouth when the hospital wouldn't let David out. I was like a wildcat, pushed into a fight I didn't want, but there was no choice but to fight. David needed me, he couldn't fight his own battles, and he needed me to fight them for him. I wasn't going to let him down. But those fights take a little more out of you each time. The battle weariness of a long struggle is real and I can't tell you how important it is to recognise that and give yourself space to come to terms with what you have done. I rarely had time to process what had happened before having to be strong for David to recover.

I had times when I used to ask myself how I got into this situation and how on earth was I grown up enough to cope with this, but somehow you do. But I have also learned that I need time to process, to bounce back like that Weeble. Whilst amid the hideousness I didn't have time, now I am learning to make time for myself. Because if I don't, I am not healing.

You will have anger, let it pass

I was angry, I got angry, and I get angry. My anger and frustration still lie very close to the surface and flares up more quickly than it ever did. I hated that the best years of my life were spent caring, that I didn't have an intimate relationship with my husband, that David couldn't be the father that George needed, and that God took David.

But I am learning to separate the anger into things that I can't change and things that I can. But all the time the emotions come and go – I have learned to understand that cycles of emotion only last longer if you choose to engage with the emotion. You don't have to stay angry or annoyed. You can let that emotion pass; the sun will always come out again if you give it chance. Life is too short to stay angry.

Humour takes many forms, use it

A black sense of humour sprang up on possibly the most inappropriate of moments. Shortly after David was on hospital on George's birthday Brandy, our old dog, went into the vets for some exploratory procedures as he was having some problems breathing. He had to have general anaesthetic and I remember saying to the vet that if it was something cancerous that he would suffer from, then put him down rather than have him in pain. At which point I started laughing and told the vet that I had had the same conversation with David's surgeon about three weeks before. I found it very funny, but I could hear the baffled silence of incomprehension at the other end of the phone! I have spoken to many people in the similar situations, and this is quite common. Do what you feel is right; quite often the sense of humour stops you from going completely mad so if you need to laugh, then laugh!

Support others and pay it forward

Everyone has a life story and a lot of people need help. I have found the more I can be open with the situations that George and I have faced, the more rewarding the situation we find ourselves in. It not only helps me come to terms with what has happened, but it also helps other people cope. The Facebook group that I was on, 'We are the Wives of GBM and this is our story', was possibly the most supportive group. If I can pay that forward by supporting others, I will.

I've found that people are making the best decisions that they can, no-one intentionally makes a bad call. If we can suspend judgment and support others we will live in a more understanding and compassionate society. A physician doesn't make the wrong decision on purpose, and someone at work doesn't try and do a job badly. If we can learn to take a deep breath before reacting we might have a chance to make our world better.

Everyone has had a past, a life

My past is not stamped on my forehead and knowledge of my hurt does not precede me – how do people know and why should they? I am much more accepting of everyone's past and take them for what they are. My fundamental belief is that everything happens for a reason and everything happened me to, happened purposefully. And if that is the case, it would be exceedingly arrogant to believe that I am the only one. So, in accepting my past, then I have learned to accept others and, in turn, to help those around me accept what has happened to them. Gentleness and open arms will always triumph, love will always win, light will always find a way through the cracks.

Spend time with your tribe

You don't have to be related by blood to be a family member. As Louisa says, everyone finds their 'tribe'. I never spent enough time with David. I remember sitting on a meeting watching David having a seizure in the lounge and thinking 'I've got a bit of time yet'. I am shaking my head as I write this. What mindset was I in when I thought that was an OK thing to think? Why did I work to the week of his death and go back to work before his funeral? I am trying to learn to get perspective on time and what is important in life. I am not talking about a work-life balance as work is part of life, but genuine perspective. Time with no distractions. And when you find that time, cherish every moment and tell your family how much you appreciate and love them. Hug hard.

Behind Closed Doors

This is possibly the most important lesson. No one knows what is happening behind closed doors. No one. David put a very different face on for people outside than inside the house. As did I. As do I still. The countless times that people said how surprised they were about how well David looked, how well we were coping, that you wouldn't know anything was wrong. People have no idea what is happening and their words are there for comfort. But in the same way that people didn't know what was happening in our house, neither do I know what is happening in anyone else's. So, I try to suspend judgement, I try to hold people gently, I try to see behind people's smile.

When all is said and done, you can't go too far wrong with being gentle, being kind, being loving.

You can be the person who helps someone choose to float.

.

Appendix Two

DAVID'S EULOGY

.

DAVID'S EULOGY

Read by me on 12th June 2021, All Saint Church, North Molton.

David managed to stand up and do eulogies for both his Mum and Dad and do Father of the Bride for Karen so there is absolutely no chance that he is going to beat me on this – so here I am doing David!

David Campbell (David, never Dave) was born in Northern Ireland (Northern Ireland never Ireland) and he loved his home and his heritage. He loved Newtownabbey, the bonfires, Windsor Park, Glengormley High, Ulster table tennis and the Windy Hill Road and it was a blessing that we were able to travel over in May. Family was of utmost importance to David (although many here would probably doubt that considering his appalling track record of not replying to texts or answering his phone) - sense the frustration! According to David's parents.... especially Lena who was frequently heard to say, beaming with pride - "my son, my son" .... David was a model child and, according to my parents, a model son-in-law. But Karen and I have rather different ideas – we know that David knew how to suck up to the parents...with emails, texts, cooking meals – he even sent flowers for heaven's sake! We were on a hiding to nothing trying to compete in the favouritism stakes!

However, David was an amazing friend, brother, son, cousin,

nephew, and soulmate.... but the relationship that was the most important to him was that of father. David was born to be a dad and he loved George with absolute devotion. Every night David walked passed George's room and, no matter what the time, said "love you George". And this devotion was right from the word "go" – When I was pregnant he spent hours with a pen torch tracking across my tummy to see if George would move. During labour our midwife said that David had missed his calling because he spent so much time down at the "business end". David did the night feeds, bedtimes, story reading, baby massage, play dates, birthday parties and later Friday Night Club trips, Campbell cabs to numerous sports...and he adored every moment of it. I don't think anyone that saw or knew David could doubt how much he loved George.

David was happiest when he was helping people (usually ladies) and flirting (anyone really). Nothing was ever too much or too little trouble. He was never happier than running errands to the shop for milk, bread, papers – any reason really to pop down and see Anne, Colin, and the team...having a chat to anyone and everyone on the way there and back. In fact, I wouldn't be surprised if he isn't up there now heading off to a celestial shop armed with list of supplies to deliver! He enjoyed cooking and washing up for Luncheon Club and I think it was never more popular than when David and Andrew were manning the kitchen. I know that I never want to see another Sticky Toffee Pudding as long as I live...David was planning it for weeks and we could have fed the whole village with the final amount made!

We have been absolutely overwhelmed with cards and love since David died and most of them mention his smile or his eyes, his hugs, his love of life or the fact that he was an inspiration to so many and I think is an amazing tribute to him and would have actually come as a surprise to David (possibly not the smiles or hugs!) And David did love life, and he lived as he knew best – in his calm, unflappable and generally horizontal approach. Taking life at his own speed and being happy in his own David world.

When we got the glioblastoma diagnosis in July 2020 and we realized that David's life was going to be shorter than we wanted, our thoughts inevitably turned to a bucket list but, typically for David, all he wanted to do was spend time with his friends and family. And we did that to the absolute best of our ability and I would like to thank everyone here today (and also many that can't attend in person) for all the wonderful times that you gave us and all the support that you have given family Campbell: whether it be endless cups of tea, skype calls, hot dates between our dogs, walks, hours milking, squeezy eyed prayers and inappropriately long hugs, lifts to football and rugby, impromptu beers in the back garden, play dates with George – the list is endless. You might not have realised how much that meant to David at the time – but it meant the world.

David never wanted fuss, pity, or any special treatment and to most of the world, our lives looked very normal, but David's frustration with his brain and toll that life generally took on him were the only reasons he got angry and frustrated. So, few people saw and understood the effort that life cost David, the hours that he would spend typing each text and email, checking how to spell so many words and then checking with me that what he put made sense and wasn't offensive (and yes, there were a few emails that slipped through the net!) But we both knew that David would go to heaven and leave all his worldly cares behind him and I thank God for our unfaltering faith.

And David's faith has been a great comfort to us both. Again, a man of few words, but some of the most memorable ones for me was when David first got diagnosed twelve years ago. Me, being me, railed against the whole thing…but after a particularly fraught conversation (probably involving wine) and me shouting "why?" David said that God had given him the tumour because he knew he could cope with it. David's faith humbled me.

It is particularly fitting that we are here today as David loved this church; it was here we got married, here where George got baptised, here where David prepared and attended services most Wednesdays, and, until lockdown, most Sundays, it's here when he couldn't drive or walk too far, where he brought Brandy and Trampus. It's this church that, in term time, David came up in the morning to unlock and evening to lock the church up. (Not with 100% hit rate admittedly!) It's here where he lit candles and prayed.

David's smile lit up his face and Karen and I were witness to the fact he saved his best smiles for his carers, nurses, and visitors in the last few weeks of his life. David approached his death with the same grace that he carried with him through life and Karen and I could see everyone respond to that. We feel that David could not have received better care, and despite these challenging times, we never felt alone or lost and we want to publicly acknowledge and say thank you to the wonderful NHS and Hospice Teams that were only ever a call (or a smile) away.

When David was diagnosed he told me that if he saw forty, he wanted the biggest party ever. His party would have been three weeks today. Karen and I were talking the other day and we can say, with our hands on our hearts, that David would not want us to be unhappy. So, let's leave our tears in the church, raise a glass to his 40th birthday on 6th July and go and live our best lives!

AFTERWORD

My story is one about growing up, of having the happy ever after stripped away in one day, and about being catapulted into a world where life changing decisions needed to be made at the drop of a hat. Where the only way for my brain to know how to cope was a tsunami of adrenaline to numb me against the raw hideousness of daily life and the realisation that death is just around the corner.

Much of this book has been difficult to write as it involves me confronting some of the demons that I only usually raise with Louisa and Tash after imbibing more alcohol units than I should or after I have been particularly upset and Ian and I sit down to piece together my reactions.

My relationship with Ian has matured and we are now married. Ian is the opposite of David and perhaps that is what makes it work. Ian is no threat to David and my love for him. He does not try to be George's father and because he doesn't try he has a wonderful relationship with George - doing country sports and working the dogs. He supports both George and I through our grief, our anger, and our lack of being able to modulate our emotions. Ian accepts us for who we are. He once told me that he was good with injured animals and I can place my hand on my heart and say that is true. With his gentle acceptance, he is helping me find me again. The waves are still high, there are often squalls, but generally the waves are farther apart. And when they come Ian is the RNLI lifeboat that pulls alongside, to steady us before letting us set sail again. Ian is my unlooked-for blessing and I thank God daily for bringing this kind, gentle and good man into our lives. He is a miracle to me.

I've always felt there was a book in me to write mainly because, over the thirteen years that David was ill, we experienced so much. I wouldn't presume to know what anyone else is going through in their lives but if you can read this book and you gain insight, or learn something about yourself, then my work is done. It doesn't always have to be about life-limiting illness, most people have trauma in their lives at some stage, and I believe that the fundamentals are the same. No-one, without exception, will walk the same path that you will walk so go gently with how you feel and reflect where you can. At many stages throughout David's illness, I didn't want to look back or analyse, it was too painful, but now, nearly three years after David's death, I hope my insights might be of some benefit or comfort to you.

David's story is one of hope, of how light, no matter how hidden, will find a crack to pour through. How hope will bubble to the surface and how our souls found a way to heal.

David's story is a love story, a love of life, a love of the power for good, a love of light, of people, of faith, of joy, of laughter. It is basically a love of love.

My hope and prayer for you, your friends, family and loved ones, is that you will always choose to float.

God bless.
Clare.